CLEOPATRA

· THE SEARCH FOR THE LAST QUEEN OF EGYPT ·

ZAHI HAWASS *and* FRANCK GODDIO

NATIONAL GEOGRAPHIC

WASHINGTON, D.C.

A diver stares at the illuminated statue of Hapy, god of the flood of the Nile.

CONTENTS

PAGE 1: This bronze coin is one of the only contemporary likenesses of Cleopatra in existence today.
PAGE 2-3: Today the bustling Alexandrian harbor carries on Cleopatra's legacy.

The sight of Taposiris Magna at dusk evokes the romance of Cleopatra and Mark Antony, thought to be buried there.

FOREWORD

Zahi Hawass

When I first set out to become an archaeologist, the mystery of Cleopatra already mesmerized me. At age 16, I enrolled as a student with the Faculty of Arts in the Archaeology Department of the University of Alexandria. I asked Dr. Fawzi El Fakhary, one of my professors, a question that had been hovering in my mind for some time: Where was the tomb of Cleopatra? My professor believed her to be buried near her palace with Mark Antony, in a tomb long lost beneath the depths of the ocean. My professor's answer, however, was only an educated guess. He did not know where Cleopatra was buried, and this uncertainty only fueled the mounting flame of my curiosity. I used to visit the location that people thought was her palace and conjure her in my mind, marveling at how little we knew about Egypt's last queen and how much remained to be discovered.

After graduating from the university, my interest in Cleopatra waned until, in 2004, Kathleen Martinez, a Dominican scholar of Greek and Roman history, explained her theory about Cleopatra. She described her as a philosopher and linguist, and a shrewd politician—a woman to be reckoned with. Kathleen was certain that Cleopatra and Mark Antony were buried together inside the temple of Taposiris Magna, a site located 45 kilometers west of Alexandria, far from the submerged tomb my professor had described.

According to Kathleen, this temple represented the dwelling of the god Osiris, which possessed a profound meaning for Cleopatra, who frequently portrayed herself as the human representation of the goddess Isis, wife of Osiris. Mark Antony, Cleopatra's lover in the years before her death, was often seen as the human manifestation of Osiris. Thus the temple of Taposiris may have held a deeply sentimental importance for this queen, who lost Antony just before Egypt fell to the Romans.

Kathleen had searched for Cleopatra's tomb in other temples by carefully analyzing a wealth of architectural, archaeological, and iconographical evidence as well as the symbolism, chronology, and mythology surrounding these temples. The only possible burial place that embodied all the symbolism of divinity and religious ritual, while simultaneously conveying Cleopatra's personal legacy, was Taposiris Magna.

Many have searched for the tomb of Alexander the Great, but no one had searched for that missing piece of ancient Egypt's story—the tomb of Cleopatra, who took her own life rather than surrender her homeland to the Romans. This bright young scholar rekindled my old passion for the story of Cleopatra. It occurred to me that we had before us an opportunity to recover the last page in the book of ancient Egyptian civilization, an opportunity we could not pass by. And so Kathleen and I, together with an Egyptian archaeological team, began the search for Cleopatra's tomb in hopes of removing some of the great mystery that hangs thick around this famous queen. ∎

Franck Goddio

On some of my first archaeological dives in the Bay of Aboukir northeast of Alexandria, in 1984, my team and I were investigating the remains of *L'Orient,* the flagship of Napoleon's fleet that was sunk by Admiral Nelson. It soon became clear that these shallow waters of the Bay of Aboukir contained much more than a Napoleonic shipwreck. Entire underwater cityscapes lay on the seafloor, waiting to be restored to their former glory. The mystery of these waters immediately captivated me; the thought that further exploration might unlock some of the biggest questions about Egyptian history was too much for me to resist.

I knew that I would never be able to undertake an exploration of this scope by myself, and so, in 1985, I founded the European Institute of Underwater Archaeology (IEASM), an independent organization supported by private patronage. The primary goal of IEASM was to locate and excavate lost archaeological sites, and to study, restore, and present to the public the objects that underwater archaeologists discovered there. The foundation accumulated an outstanding team of archaeological divers, restoration experts, and researchers, and in 1992, with some generous donations and the permission of the Egyptian government, we began work in the ancient port of Alexandria.

Since then, IEASM research teams have uncovered exceptional works from Alexandria and the sunken cities of Canopus and Heracleion in the Bay of Aboukir. Statues of ancient Egyptian gods, sphinxes, ritual instruments, and gleaming golden vessels have been pulled up from underwater and returned to their native country. All along the streets of Aboukir and Alexandria, as the enormous statues of a Ptolemaic king and queen passed by on their way to restoration and study, crowds applauded and cried out, "Long live Ramses! Long live Cleopatra!" We were so proud to share with the Egyptians the heritage of their civilization.

Although I did not set out to search for Cleopatra, she surfaced in our excavations. Bronze coins bearing her face, ceramics and statuettes produced during her rule, and statues of Ptolemaic queens were all brought up from underwater. Cleopatra's royal palaces came to life before our eyes, as we developed the first map of the ancient Alexandrian port based on the structures we analyzed underwater.

As our work revealed more clues to Cleopatra's life and times, I became more and more curious about this woman who was a permanent fixture in the collective imagination of Egypt and the world. Although I stumbled upon my search for this ancient queen, I, too, found myself inspired by her mystery, driven to keep searching for elements of her life in hopes that we might someday understand why she emerged as the most memorable queen of the entire Mediterranean, and why it is that we still know so little about her. ∎

SEARCHING FOR CLEOPATRA

LAST PHARAOH of the PTOLEMIES

Zahi Hawass

The young princess Cleopatra VII, known today as simply Cleopatra, became queen of Egypt in the year 51 B.C. Thrust onto the world stage by her father, Ptolemy XII, she ruled a country in tumult, one on the verge of crumbling under the mighty Roman Empire. Only 17 years old when she took the throne, Cleopatra quickly became one of the most powerful rulers Egypt had ever known. She bonded personally and politically with two of ancient Rome's most powerful leaders, Julius Caesar and Mark Antony. Then, barely two decades after coming to power, this queen took her own life in a climactic act of defiance against the Romans, still hungry for her kingdom.

While we know these facts of Cleopatra's life and times, much remains to be discovered. Who was Cleopatra, really? What, and whom, did she hold dear? Was she the exotic beauty depicted by modern artists and filmmakers, or did she lure her famous lovers with her intelligence and power? From the underwater ruins of the once vibrant Alexandria to the desert remains of a temple where she may have gone to begin her journey into the afterlife, archaeologists today seek further evidence about the life, death, and world of Egypt's last queen. Still, ever since, Cleopatra has remained shrouded in the layers of history, revealing just enough to captivate the world's imagination.

The kneeling figure incised on this plaque raises his arms in celebration. The sun disk above his head symbolizes the eternal daily cycle of the sun.

PREVIOUS PAGES: Divers clear a 26th-dynasty pharaoh's head from the seafloor sediment.

EGYPT BEFORE THE PTOLEMIES

The colossal Pyramids at Giza, now the universal symbol of ancient Egypt, had already existed for thousands of years before Cleopatra's royal line, the Ptolemaic dynasty, came to power. These remarkable structures were built around 2600 B.C.,

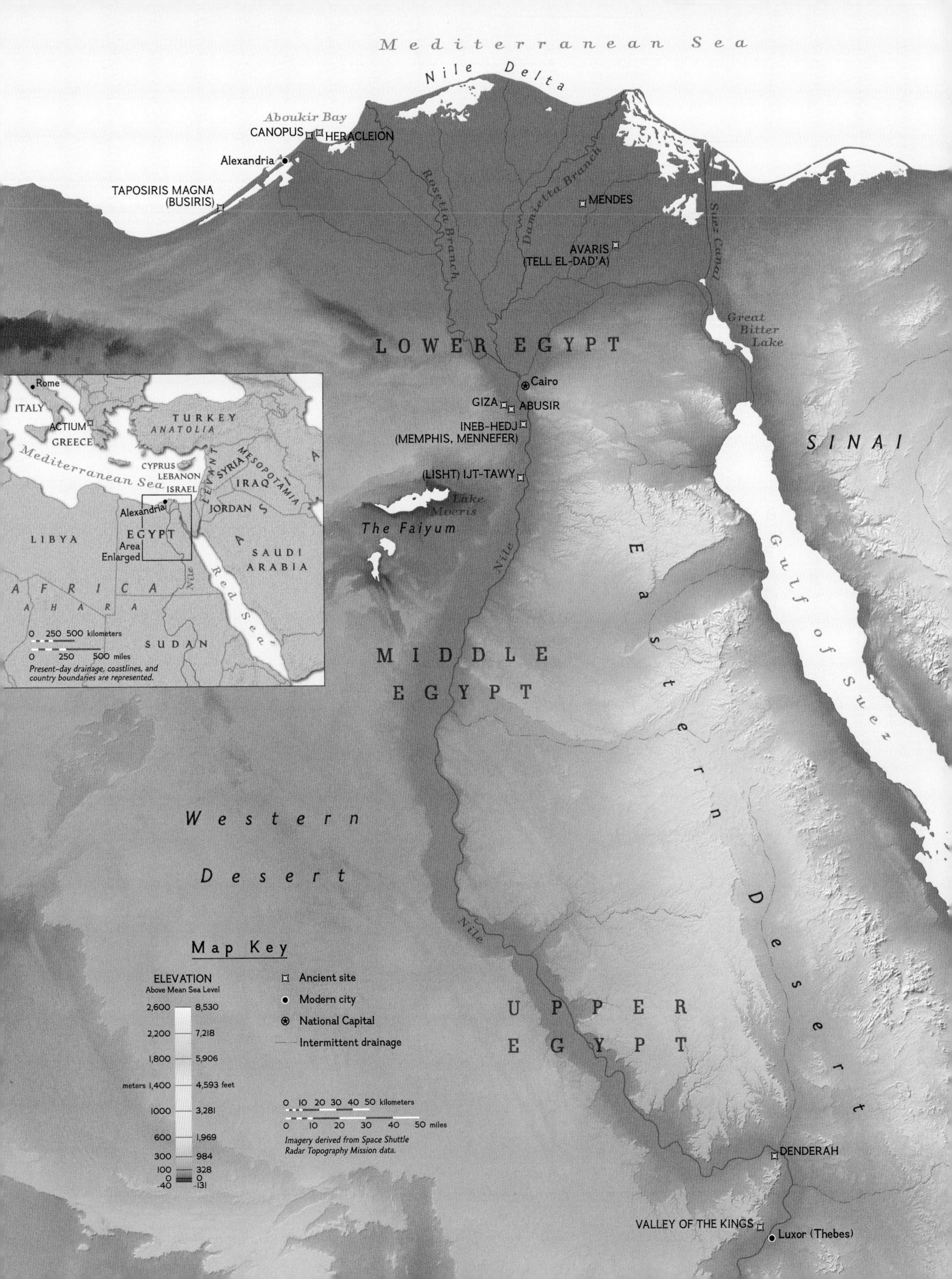

Mediterranean Sea
Nile Delta
Aboukir Bay
CANOPUS
HERACLEION
Alexandria
TAPOSIRIS MAGNA
(BUSIRIS)
Rosetta Branch
Damietta Branch
MENDES
AVARIS
(TELL EL-DAD'A)
Suez Canal
Great Bitter Lake
LOWER EGYPT
Cairo
GIZA
ABUSIR
INEB-HEDJ
(MEMPHIS, MENNEFER)
(LISHT) IJT-TAWY
Lake Moeris
The Faiyum
SINAI
Gulf of Suez
Nile
Eastern Desert
MIDDLE EGYPT
Western Desert
UPPER EGYPT
DENDERAH
VALLEY OF THE KINGS
Luxor (Thebes)
Rome
ITALY
ACTIUM
GREECE
TURKEY
ANATOLIA
Mediterranean Sea
CYPRUS
LEBANON
ISRAEL
LEVANT
SYRIA
MESOPOTAMIA
IRAQ
JORDAN
Alexandria
EGYPT
Area Enlarged
LIBYA
SAUDI ARABIA
AFRICA
SAHARA
Nile
Red Sea
SUDAN
0 250 500 kilometers
0 250 500 miles
Present-day drainage, coastlines, and country boundaries are represented.
Map Key
ELEVATION
Above Mean Sea Level
meters
feet
2,600 8,530
2,200 7,218
1,800 5,906
1,400 4,593
1000 3,281
600 1,969
300 984
100 328
0 0
-40 -131
Ancient site
Modern city
National Capital
Intermittent drainage
0 10 20 30 40 50 kilometers
0 10 20 30 40 50 miles
Imagery derived from Space Shuttle Radar Topography Mission data.

The black stone queen with inlaid eyes gazes out on her underwater domain.

during a period of history commonly referred to as the Old Kingdom. After periods of instability, including a time when the Hyksos, an Asiatic people, ruled Egypt for 150 years, King Ahmose I became the pharaoh, initiating the New Kingdom, a golden age that saw Egypt come into its own as a powerful empire.

After almost 500 years, the empire held under the New Kingdom was lost, and Egypt moved into a new era of fragmentation, the Third Intermediate Period. In the mid-eighth century B.C., a dynasty from the Nubian kingdom of Kush, far to the south, conquered Egypt. At the beginning of the seventh century B.C., the kingdom of Ashur (present-day Iraq) took Egypt from the Nubians and was immediately challenged by the native 26th dynasty, inaugurating the Late Period. During the 26th or Saite dynasty, increasing numbers of Greek merchants entered Egypt and established trading posts in the delta. With the new wealth from increasing Greek trade, Egypt's king, Psamtik, began promoting Greek soldiers and merchants within the Egyptian army to help him establish and maintain his power. As the stability of Egypt increased, Psamtik cultivated relations with the Mediterranean world.

In about 525 B.C., the Persian influence in Egypt also increased. Persian king Cambyses defeated the Egyptians at Pelusium, in the Sinai. In order to legitimize his reign in Egypt, he took the title of pharaoh, even though he—and most of the Persian kings who followed him—did not respect the ancient Egyptian religion. Soon the Persians controlled all of Egypt. They were harsh rulers scornful of local beliefs and customs, and their Egyptian subjects rebelled against them. Persian rule in Egypt ended in November 332 B.C., when Alexander the Great of Macedonia conquered Egypt. Alexander went to Memphis, Egypt's oldest capital, where he mingled with the Egyptians and made offerings to their gods. Afterward, he journeyed to the delta, founding the new city of Alexandria, which then became Egypt's capital city.

This squat lekythos has a round foot, a globular body, and a palmette decoration. This type of pottery was a popular import from Attica in the fourth and fifth centuries B.C.

Alexander understood that he needed to respect the local religion if he wanted loyalty from his subjects. According to Egyptian religion, the last true god-king was Horus, the child of Re, the sun god. The pharaoh represented Horus on earth, meaning that he or she was both a god and the child of a god. He or she was also a high priest, the only person who could connect with both the gods and the deceased. These ideas of the divine right of kingship had existed since the Early Predynastic Period, and every pharaoh's power was deeply rooted in religion. According to tradition, the kings were gods who controlled the land, taught the arts of life, and established the rules of religion. Eventually the Egyptians came to revere Alexander as they would have revered one of their own deities.

EGYPT UNDER THE PTOLEMIES

After Alexander's death, Ptolemy I, who was one of his generals, gained control of Egypt. We do not know much about Ptolemy's origins, except that he, like Alexander, was raised in the Macedonian court of King Philip II, the father of Alexander the Great, and was a good friend of Alexander's from the beginning years of his life. Ptolemy I designated Alexandria the capital of his Egypt. His reign represents the beginning of the Ptolemaic dynasty, which lasted from 304 B.C. to 30 B.C. and ended with the death of Cleopatra, the last of Egypt's Ptolemaic rulers.

The Ptolemaic kings and queens were not native to Egypt. They were from Macedonia, the ancient name for a region in today's northeastern Greece. They followed Alexander's precedent, nevertheless, and, unlike the Persian rulers before them, respected the beliefs of the Egyptians, who believed that the pharaoh was the source of life and owner of all land. The Ptolemies continued to fulfill this role, emphasizing their rights as divine kings within that tradition. The Ptolemaic rulers became "Egyptianized" by worshipping Egyptian gods, supporting the temple priests, and donning the titles given to pharaohs. Ptolemy I took two titles of the pharaohs; beginning with Ptolemy II, the kings used all five of the traditional pharaonic titles.

A painting from between 1470 and 1483 entitled "The Deaths of Antony and Cleopatra" shows not one, but two serpents biting Cleopatra's breast as Mark Antony stabs himself alongside his beloved.

Foreign ministers under the Ptolemies focused on securing the borders against attack from outside. Many people in the army and administration hailed from Macedon and Greece, and Jewish, Syrian, Phoenician, and Libyan immigrants all lived side by side with the Egyptians. Ptolemy I increased the wealth of Egypt and improved relations between the Greeks and the Egyptians. He won the Greeks over by building temples for Greek gods, giving them land, and deifying Alexander the Great.

Plutarch, one of the greatest of the Greek and Roman historians and an important source for the history of Greece and Rome up to the first century A.D., recorded that Ptolemy I appointed a group of intellectuals to meet and found a new way for everyone to worship together. They created a sacred triad composed of the god Serapis (a later interpretation of Osiris), the goddess Isis, and their son Harpocrates. Isis was clearly an Egyptian goddess, and many believed that Serapis and Osiris, the Egyptian god of the afterlife, were the same. Harpocrates was the Greek form of the Egyptian Horus. Egyptians and Greeks alike joined in worship of this triad. When Cleopatra came into power, she associated herself with Isis, the sole female of this sacred trinity.

Ptolemy I encouraged the spread of the Egyptian religion. He gave funds for the festival of the sacred bull and rebuilt the holy of holies in the temple of Karnak. Ptolemy II Philadelphos built many temples to show his respect for the Egyptian religion, and docu-

The goddess Isis depicted as a cobra, a popular motif in Roman Alexandria, was closely associated with Cleopatra.

ments reveal the care Ptolemy III and his wife, Berenike, gave to the temples and the sacred animals, appointing priests and bringing back statues of the pharaohs that had been stolen by the Persians. They also rebuilt important temples on the sites of earlier monuments.

The Ptolemies used Egyptian priests to keep the country stable, but they also looked for ways to control them and curtail their power. By placing the administration of the temples under the state, the Ptolemies could levy taxes on them, crippling their economic independence.

During the Ptolemaic period, Greeks held positions of power, while Egyptians were appointed only to lower-level positions. Greek was the language of the ruling elites, but Egyptians continued to speak their native tongue. At this time, there was one set of laws

Underwater archaeologist Franck Goddio illuminates the foundation plaque of Ptolemy III.

for Egyptians, another for foreigners, and a third for those who lived in Greek cities within Egypt. Each set of laws had its own courts and judges. Over time, as the Ptolemaic rulers grew weaker, the Egyptians gained more rights in the army, court, and administration, ultimately gaining enough power to revolt against their Ptolemaic leaders.

Agriculture, manufacturing, and trade supported the economy under the Ptolemies. The majority of the agricultural land was controlled by the king and rented to farmers. Temple complexes took up significant amounts of land as well, and Ptolemaic leaders began taking over that land in order to control the power of the priests. Oil, salt, and textiles were important industries, but the most important was papyrus, made for export.

From the time of Ptolemy II, during the third century B.C., Romans began importing Egyptian wheat, giving the Roman Empire a commercial incentive to ensure Egypt's political stability. Rome played an increasingly large role in Egyptian politics during the Ptolemaic period, an important ally at some points but a threat to independence as well. In 202 B.C., after the victory of Rome in the Second Punic War, a mission came to Egypt, headed by Roman Marcus Lidius, starting rumors that Lidius was going to be placed in charge of Egypt. But Rome only wanted to keep Egypt safe from the rule of others.

Found in 2003 amid the ruins of Heracleion, this plaque contains Ptolemy III's dedication of a gymnasium to the god Heracles.

When Ptolemy VI Philometor took the throne in 180 B.C., at the age of 15, Antiochus, the king of Syria, decided to attack. To prevent Syria from expanding

its empire in Egypt, the Romans moved in: one more step in Egypt's loss of independence. From this point forward, weak Ptolemaic kings were controlled by Rome, paying half the country's income in taxes and taking direction from the emperor and senate.

Instability pervaded Egypt when Cleopatra was born. Her father, Ptolemy XII, came to power after the king and queen before him were murdered. Commonly known as "Auletes," or the Flutist, Ptolemy XII depended on the goodwill of Rome. He spent Egyptian money to bribe Rome, which infuriated the people of Alexandria to such an extent that they revolted against him in 58 B.C. Ptolemy XII fled to Rome, where he so ingratiated himself to certain powerful leaders that they eventually helped him return to Egypt and his throne.

Resuming his position of power, Ptolemy XII punished those Alexandrians who had rebelled against him. He had his daughter Berenice IV, Cleopatra's older sister, put to death because she had ascended to the throne in his absence. Yet he wanted to guarantee that his children would be his successors, and so in 51 B.C. Ptolemy XII wrote a will granting the throne to 17-year-old Cleopatra and mandating that she share power with her younger brother, Ptolemy XIII, around 11 years old at the time. The elder ruler kept the original will in Alexandria and sent a copy to Rome, asking his Roman friends to enforce it if need be. Thus, upon his death, Cleopatra VII, 13th in the line of the Ptolemies, became the pharaoh of Egypt, the last of her line to do so.

Dating to Egypt's Ptolemaic period, this amulet has the shape of a temple.

CLEOPATRA'S WORLD

Four cities formed the landscape of Cleopatra's world: Alexandria, Canopus, Heracleion, and Taposiris Magna. Alexandria was the capital, the royal city, a place of importance not just for Egypt but for the entire Mediterranean world. Ancient Alexandria was designed to have five districts, each named with a letter of the Greek alphabet. Alpha was the royal area that included the palaces, temples, museums, libraries, and gardens. Beta was the area of the Greek aristocrats. Gamma was the area where other Greek citizens lived; Delta was for foreigners—Syrians, Jews, and Persians; and Epsilon was where Egyptian citizens lived. The famous lighthouse, one of the wonders of the ancient world, was begun by Ptolemy I and finished in the reign of Ptolemy II. Made of limestone, granite, and marble, it stood more than 100 meters tall on Pharos Island, on the outer edge of the harbor, and guided trading ships safely into port from

Archaeologists believe that they will soon uncover the tomb of Cleopatra and Mark Antony at the site of Taposiris Magna.

The face of a granodiorite pharaoh displays one of the traditional crowns of Egyptian rulers.

tens, even hundreds, of miles away. A bronze statue of Poseidon, Greek god of the sea, stood atop its dome.

At the time of Cleopatra, Alexandria had become a center of politics and commerce, as well as the cultural capital of the Mediterranean. The Royal Library of Alexandria, founded during the third century B.C. and a center of literature and learning, contained books in Greek, Egyptian, Hebrew, Phoenician, and other contemporary languages. Scientists from all over the world flocked to Egypt's capital, making this city a hub of scientific learning.

While Alexandria to this day commands an important place on the Mediterranean coastline, some of the more important cities of Cleopatra's world have disappeared over time. Northeast of Alexandria lay the city of Canopus, recently located in the Bay of Aboukir through the underwater archaeological explorations of Franck Goddio. Canopus was a center of spiritual life for the Egyptians; many of the most important religious processions and rituals took place within the bounds of the city. At the same time, Canopus was infamous as the site of lavish festivals. Cleopatra and Mark Antony are said to have visited this city so that their love affair could blossom beyond the critical eye of Roman and Egyptian officials.

Heracleion, another locale lost in time and rediscovered through underwater archaeology, sat at the mouth of a major tributary of the Nile and served as a port of entry into Egypt. Cleopatra was likely crowned in the famed temple at Heracleion, a city whose Greek population made it one of the most important Greek trading centers in the Mediterranean. More significant even than Alexandria in the days of Cleopatra, Heracleion was an inspiration to the last queen of Egypt, who developed her royal Alexandria into an equally important flourishing commercial center.

Standing nearly 47 kilometers west of Alexandria, Taposiris Magna was an important religious center in Cleopatra's day. Founded by Ptolemy II in the third century B.C., it had become the site of a major temple to Osiris, husband to Isis, by around 25 B.C., based on reports by the Greek historian Strabo. Built along the coastal drive between the

A diver shows the name of the city of Thonis on a stela from King Nectanebo I, found at the site of Heracleion.

This ceramic vase is characteristic of Sicilian pottery exported throughout the Mediterranean in the fourth century B.C. It has a deep convex bowl and an intricate depiction of a female follower of Dionysus, the Greek god identified with Osiris by the Egyptians.

Mediterranean and a freshwater lake, the temple site, today called Abousir, was named Busiris by the ancient Greeks—another link to Osiris, whose body was believed to lie there.

In the search for Cleopatra, these four locations—Alexandria, Canopus, Heracleion, and Taposiris Magna—hold the most promise. Excavations in all four areas are uncovering clues that give us ever clearer answers to the mystery of who she was and what her life and world were like.

THE SEARCH BEGINS

From political history to religious customs, we have a rough sketch of the Egyptian world around the time Cleopatra entered it. We know the most important industries of Egypt's economy, and the sacred triad of deities that Greeks and Egyptians joined together to worship. We know which urban centers were most important, and we know of the terrible murders that caused this queen's rise to the throne. We also know about the precarious political and economic plight of her country at the time. The more closely we examine this picture, the more we return to the questions that have been left unanswered, the questions that tantalize us with their ambiguity, making Cleopatra the charismatic, yet enigmatic, figure she is today.

And so we search for answers, in the sunken city of Alexandria, in the remains of Canopus and Heracleion, and in the temple ruins of Taposiris Magna, which may prove to hold the tomb of the great queen. Accompany my colleague, Franck Goddio, and me as we share the work we are pursuing. Follow along as you learn what sort of instruments accompanied the royal processions Cleopatra attended, what types of statues lined the temple walls through which she strode. Come with us as we unearth the gold jewelry that Cleopatra might have worn and bring to light the calendar by which she may have counted her days.

Immerse yourself in this amazing world and share in the excitement of the never ending search for Cleopatra, last queen of Egypt. ∎

THE LINE OF THE PTOLEMIES

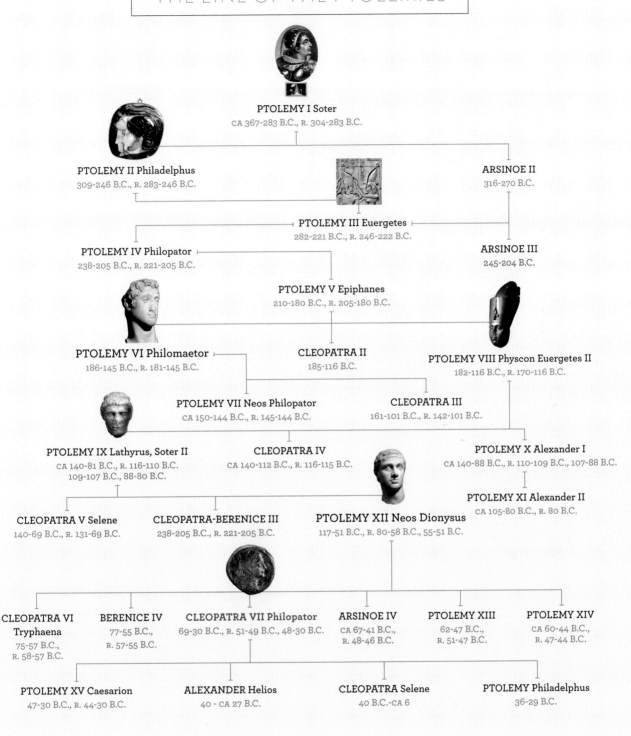

PTOLEMY I Soter
CA 367-283 B.C., R. 304-283 B.C.

PTOLEMY II Philadelphus
309-246 B.C., R. 283-246 B.C.

ARSINOE II
316-270 B.C.

PTOLEMY III Euergetes
282-221 B.C., R. 246-222 B.C.

PTOLEMY IV Philopator
238-205 B.C., R. 221-205 B.C.

ARSINOE III
245-204 B.C.

PTOLEMY V Epiphanes
210-180 B.C., R. 205-180 B.C.

PTOLEMY VI Philomaetor
186-145 B.C., R. 181-145 B.C.

CLEOPATRA II
185-116 B.C.

PTOLEMY VIII Physcon Euergetes II
182-116 B.C., R. 170-116 B.C.

PTOLEMY VII Neos Philopator
CA 150-144 B.C., R. 145-144 B.C.

CLEOPATRA III
161-101 B.C., R. 142-101 B.C.

PTOLEMY IX Lathyrus, Soter II
CA 140-81 B.C., R. 116-110 B.C.
109-107 B.C., 88-80 B.C.

CLEOPATRA IV
CA 140-112 B.C., R. 116-115 B.C.

PTOLEMY X Alexander I
CA 140-88 B.C., R. 110-109 B.C., 107-88 B.C.

PTOLEMY XI Alexander II
CA 105-80 B.C., R. 80 B.C.

CLEOPATRA V Selene
140-69 B.C., R. 131-69 B.C.

CLEOPATRA-BERENICE III
238-205 B.C., R. 221-205 B.C.

PTOLEMY XII Neos Dionysus
117-51 B.C., R. 80-58 B.C., 55-51 B.C.

CLEOPATRA VI
Tryphaena
75-57 B.C.,
R. 58-57 B.C.

BERENICE IV
77-55 B.C.,
R. 57-55 B.C.

CLEOPATRA VII Philopator
69-30 B.C., R. 51-49 B.C., 48-30 B.C.

ARSINOE IV
CA 67-41 B.C.,
R. 48-46 B.C.

PTOLEMY XIII
62-47 B.C.,
R. 51-47 B.C.

PTOLEMY XIV
CA 60-44 B.C.,
R. 47-44 B.C.

PTOLEMY XV Caesarion
47-30 B.C., R. 44-30 B.C.

ALEXANDER Helios
40 - CA 27 B.C.

CLEOPATRA Selene
40 B.C.-CA 6

PTOLEMY Philadelphus
36-29 B.C.

CHAPTER ONE

SUNKEN CITIES

THE UNDERWATER WORLD of
CLEOPATRA

Franck Goddio

or centuries, ancient writers had praised the Egyptian cities of Canopus and Heracleion as visions of splendor. Such descriptions had long sparked the interest of historians and archaeologists in the modern world, but the cities themselves were nowhere to be found. Finally, in 1992, researchers from the Institut Européen d'Archéologie Sous-Marine—European Institute of Underwater Archaeology (IEASM)—set out to search the Alexandrian waters. Literary texts, ancient inscriptions, papyrological documentation, and archaeological information provided by Egypt's Supreme Council of Antiquities (SCA) all indicated great promise in this region. Still, scientists had only a faint idea of the monuments and artifacts hidden in these shallow waters. Their discoveries now reveal that Canopus and Heracleion formed a rich network with nearby Alexandria, a network that allowed the entire region to flourish. Today the sunken cities contain only remnants of this network, but artifact by artifact, excavations have brought us a few steps closer in the never ending search for Cleopatra VII, the last Ptolemaic queen of Egypt.

The quest undertaken by IEASM was not the first exploration along the Alexandrian coast and the Bay of Aboukir to the northeast. One notable discovery occurred in 1933, when Group Captain Cull, commander of the Royal Air Force Base of Aboukir, thought he glimpsed ruins while taking off from the military aerodrome. The commander alerted Prince Omar Toussoun, a knowledgeable scholar of the Nile Delta, who promptly went to the site. Finding nothing, he asked some local fishermen if they had any knowledge of submerged ruins. The prince followed their directions and located an important archaeological deposit 1.8 kilometers from the shore, comprised, so he reported, of marble columns and probably red granite. A diver sent to the location brought up something that exceeded

Toussoun's wildest dreams: the head of a white marble statue representing Alexander the Great. This discovery proved that part of the inhabited area of ancient Egypt now lay submerged beneath the sea. There was still an ancient underwater world yet to be discovered.

FINDING THE SUNKEN CITIES

Decades later, the IEASM study began. Its mission was to determine the ancient topography of the currently submerged zones of Alexandria and Canopus. Scientists performed a geophysical and geological survey using sonar and other technical instruments designed to analyze the contours of the ocean floor. The study covered 400 hectares in Alexandria and 110 square kilometers in the Bay of Aboukir. Never before had there been an archaeological study of submerged sites on such a scale, and researchers adapted their methodologies to accommodate such a large study area. To supplement their tools, they examined literary, epigraphic, and iconographical sources with clues to the mysteries of these ancient urban centers. They then contextualized their findings by referring to the historical documentation left by the region's first explorers. In the end, this study detailed how the regions of Alexandria and Canopus sank underwater as the result of rising sea levels, as well as cataclysmic events like tidal waves and earthquakes.

Researchers also had to develop ways to conserve the delicate artifacts that had been lost underwater for thousands of years. Objects long submerged in saltwater can become severely damaged upon returning to the open air, and thus conservation became the primary concern of the IEASM operation. Although removing delicate objects from the ocean required the utmost skill from scientists underwater, their true work began after these artifacts were exposed to air and brought aboard their ship. Divers recovered hundreds of objects large and small made of such diverse materials as bronze, ceramics, potteries, and various stones, and each of these materials had to be treated differently. Objects can crack or shrink if they aren't handled correctly, and pressure due to saline crystallization can also damage exposed artifacts. So first, in order to stabilize the artifacts and protect them from damage, investigators had to store them in a humid environment, where they remained until they could be transferred to the laboratory in Alexandria.

In the laboratory, scientists identified and sorted the objects according to their materials and then bathed them in distilled water. They completed conservation reports for each object, detailing the methods required to return the object to its original state. For metal objects, they used an ultrasound treatment to remove compacted layers of accumulated debris without damaging the ancient metal and then applied a chemical coating to prevent corrosion. Pottery and glass objects were allowed to dry very slowly to prevent cracking or shattering. Stone objects were cleaned with pincers and a special solution to remove mold and algae. Slowly, the objects recaptured the appearances they had in the past.

MAPPING THE ANCIENT PAST

In addition to revealing these ancient artifacts, the IEASM discoveries ultimately filled in a once incomplete picture of the ports, anchorages, and ancient sites surrounding Alexandria and the important cities nearby. In Alexandria, scientists used ancient Greek and Latin texts and a series of earlier discoveries to draw a map of the eastern port, which helped them visualize the complex of structures that made up the Ptolemaic palaces. Within these very walls, in the first century B.C., Cleopatra dreamt of developing Alexandria into a metropolis that would rival Rome. According to Plutarch, Cleopatra's royal quarters began at Cape Lochias, which wrapped around the ancient harbor to the east and included a temple to the goddess Isis.

Man-made breakwaters and a long protective wall provided protection for the port of Alexandria—"hid it from men's sight," according to the ancient geographer Strabo. The royal quarters included Antirhodos, a completely paved island that was the private property of the Ptolemaic rulers, whose ruins were discovered by IEASM researchers in an entirely different location from that imagined by historians. A central channel stretching 300 meters in length encircled an immense esplanade facing the Caesarium, Cleopatra's monument to her great love, Julius Caesar. The peninsula of the Poseidium, the temple of Poseidon, formed an arc of land extending into the port with a protective breakwater at its northernmost point. The remains of a temple from the Roman period have been excavated where the peninsula meets the ancient shoreline.

At the end of a wall of the peninsula, extending toward the center of a port basin, excavations have revealed foundations dating from the end of the first century B.C. The identity of the ruins is not certain, but according to Strabo, Mark Antony built the Timonium, a small palace-retreat at the end of a wall of the Poseidium. He wanted to retreat there and live in seclusion after his defeat at Actium by his rival Octavius. Current excavations may reveal that these ruins are, in fact, those of the famous Roman general's retreat.

The Ptolemaic dynasty built this Alexandrian harbor and its famous lighthouse, one of the Seven Wonders of the Ancient World. The remarkably preserved structures found by IEASM researchers add significant information about the building conventions of the Ptolemaic era. Blocks of limestone occur rarely, while blocks of harder rock are abundant. In fact, the submerged royal quarters of Alexandria greatly resemble the sites of the great stone temples of Lower Egypt, suggesting that stones were taken from ancient monuments and incorporated into new structures during the Ptolemaic and Roman periods. Three fragments of an obelisk, a pedestal, and a statue dating from the 13th century B.C. and several elements of a building constructed during the 6th century B.C. represent remains of monuments from pre-Alexandrian dynasties that were subsequently reused to build royal Alexandria.

The underwater research in the waters off Alexandria has also made it possible to outline the ancient boundaries of Canopus and Heracleion, locating major archaeological objects in the larger region and mapping the course of the ancient western branch of the Nile

"The place was like a temple of luxury, the likes of which would be difficult to build even in a more corrupt period; the panelled vaults were laden with riches; thick strips of gold hid the wooden pieces.... The marble was whole, and made the residence shine.... Everywhere in the palace was a profusion of onyx on which people walked."

— LUCAN, *PHARSALIA* (circa A.D. 64)

that connected these three cities. Ages ago, the cities of Canopus and Heracleion prospered as sites for worship, festivals, and trade. The veil of mystery hanging over these lost cities of Egypt lifted further with every dive carried out by members of the IEASM team. The major archaeological sites have been located and identified and remarkable objects have been found, but there are still decades of excavation and study to be conducted. All that has been found underwater and mapped or brought to view enriches our knowledge of Egyptian delta history, but every discovery also raises many more questions in the search for Cleopatra and her world. ■

PAGES 28-29: This forest of columns discovered in Canopus undoubtedly belonged to a religious building.

■ Capital

Red granite | circa A.D. 100–250
H. 85 cm | W. 130 cm | D. 130 cm

The first of two capitals excavated in the
Alexandrian harbor, this elegant piece is
similar to those found at the temples of
Serapis. Although one boss has been broken
off, the simple folds of the acanthus leaves
still evoke the stateliness of the structure this
capital once supported.

■ Capital

Red granite | circa A.D. 250–350
H. 50 cm | W. 68 cm | D. 68 cm

Sharply pointed acanthus leaves fold outward
from the collar of this Corinthian capital. Also
recovered from Alexandria's harbor, this piece
is consistent with architectural styles of the
Roman period, and the hard granite used was
common in capitals built during the Ptolemaic
and Roman periods.

Column engraved with a Greek inscription

Red granite | Caracalla, 3rd c. A.D.
H. 150 cm | Diam. 105 cm

This column includes an inscription that covers an area 113 centimeters. Although about 20 letters have been effaced and the date is illegible, the inscription clearly references the god Serapis, as well as the people of Rome and Alexandria.

Column engraved with a Greek inscription

Red granite | Caracalla, 3rd c. A.D.
H. 160 cm | Diam. 105 cm

The Greek inscription engraved on the column below covers an area 110 centimeters wide. Translated, the column reads: "[In honor of the] master of the earth and the sea and of all the inhabited world, sovereign of the universe, worshipper of Serapis, living eternally, M[arcus] Aur[elius] Severus Antoninus [. . .] Phamenoth 25 [March 25]."

Column engraved with a Greek inscription

Red granite | Caracalla, 3rd c. A.D.
H. 155 cm | Diam. 105 cm

The 95-centimeter Greek inscription on the column above begins by honoring "the master of the earth and the sea, worshipper of Serapis." This phrase is characteristic of many inscriptions from the time of Emperor Caracalla, and it emphasizes his devotion to Serapis, the god of health and well-being.

A diver peers into the depths of a crevice in the seabed.

Statue of a draped male

Red granite | Ptolemaic period
H. 120 cm | W. 40 cm | D. 31 cm

This red granite statue is of a man
standing with his left leg forward, in
accordance with compositional trends
of the Ptolemaic period. His garb also
characterizes a style of clothing unique
to that era.

The draped bodies of these Ptolemaic males, carved in red granite and granodiorite, have been remarkably preserved. The surfaces of both statues are worn, and they are both missing part of their legs and heads; nevertheless, they exemplify the artistic conventions and the customary dress of the Ptolemaic period.

This genre of statue was most popular during Cleopatra's age, the later part of the Ptolemaic era. Artists generally portrayed these men with their left foot forward and the right arm next to the side, with the thumb covering the clenched right fist. The left forearm crosses the midsection horizontally. In the case of the red granite statue, the figure is depicted as life-size, also a common approach taken by artists of the time.

Traditional three-piece garments, composed of tunic, cloak, and shawl, hang from the bodies of both figures. The slanting folds run from the right armpit to the left thigh in two rolls. The left shoulder is covered with drapery, and the edges of the shawl hang over the left elbow. Between the legs, a smooth, jutting band represents the strip of fabric worn often in Cleopatra's time. In this fashion, the citizens of Alexandria bustled through the streets while their queen ruled from her royal palaces.

■ **Statue of a draped male**

Granodiorite | Ptolemaic period
H. 45.5 cm | W. 34.5 cm | D. 26.5 cm

The dark granite body of a draped male represents trends in sculpture popular under the Ptolemies.

Statue of a draped male

Granodiorite | Ptolemaic period
H. 152 cm | W. 52 cm | D. 33 cm

This statue, still remarkably intact, stood
in the religious enclosure at Heracleion.
Dating to around the second century B.C.,
this life-size male wears traditional three-
piece clothing. The base of the neck contains
a hole, likely a reparation attempt.

▦ Torso of a benefactor

Granodiorite | Ptolemaic period
H. 42 cm | W. 30 cm | D. 15 cm

This private effigy was found at the Heracleion site.
The head and lower part of the body have disappeared,
but three hieroglyphic inscriptions adorn the chest and
upper arms. This statue demonstrates the osmosis of
Greek and Egyptian traditions in Heracleion during
the Ptolemaic period.

▦ Statue of a draped male

Granodiorite | Ptolemaic period
H. 77 cm | W. 35 cm | D. 47 cm

Only the middle section of this Ptolemaic
statue remains, but the subject's three-piece
garment is still apparent. The figure is in
motion, a departure from pharaonic
sculptural tradition.

A member of the IEASM research team raises a red granite statue of a draped male in the waters of Canopus.

Fragments of doorjamb

Red granite | 26th dynasty, Apries (589–570 B.C.)
Top portion: L. 115 cm | W. 60 cm | D. 45 cm
Lower portion: L. 150 cm | W. 60 cm | D. 45 cm

This oblong block, roughly 2.5 meters high, bears the throne name of Apries, Haa-ib-Re, pharaoh of Egypt during the 26th dynasty. In order to reuse it, the doorjamb was bisected to form a girder or beam. The hieroglyphs read: "King of Upper and Lower Egypt Haa-ib-Re, given life and power."

Inscribed block from Heliopolis

Red granite | 26th dynasty, Apries (589–570 B.C.)
L. 167 cm | W. 77 cm | D. 50 cm

Three sides of this inscribed block are preserved, and one of the sides has a hieroglyphic inscription that reads: "[Son of Re] Apries, given [life and power], [. . .] beloved of the [gods], lord of Kher-Aha."

■ Inscribed block

Red granite | 26th dynasty, Apries
(589–570 B.C.)
L. 130 cm | W. 120 cm | D. 60 cm

Minor cracks are visible on all sides
of this block, which may have been an
architrave or door lintel. On the bottom
right is a cartouche followed by the
phrase "living forever."

■ Inscribed block

Red granite | 26th dynasty, Apries
(589–570 B.C.)
L. 105 cm | W. 140 cm | D. 55 cm

The inscription on this block men-
tions the son of Atum, suggesting that
this piece originated in Heliopolis.
Theologically, this place was closely
tied to the temple of Re, the all-
important Egyptian sun god.

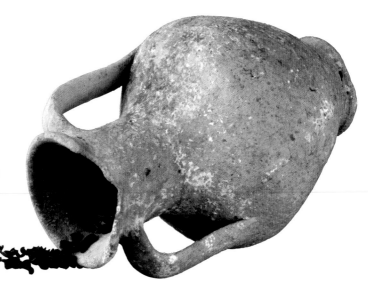

■ Table amphora

Ceramic | Mid-4th c. B.C.
H. 28.5 cm | Diam. 11 cm

Amphorae such as this were common in ancient Egypt. The rolled rim, cylindrical neck, round body, concave ring base, and handles attached under the rim are all commonly shared traits among pieces such as this one.

■ Jug

Ceramic | 2nd c. A.D.
H. 35 cm | Diam. (opening) 13.2 cm | Th. 1.6 cm

Some Alexandrian productions from the early Roman Imperial period, termed "hybrid," have ribbing similar to that seen on this jug. The rather fine working of the slim tapered body contrasts with a rather massive neck, making a crude shape indicative of hasty craftsmanship.

■ Gaza amphora

Ceramic | A.D. 4th–mid-5th c.
H. 46.5 cm | Diam. (opening) 9.5 cm | Th. 1.7 cm

Egypt maintained ongoing trade with Phoenicia, evidenced by the many amphorae found in excavations off the Egyptian coast. Hailing from the Gaza region, this small vessel was discovered in the underwater ruins of Heracleion.

The ancient town of Mende, located in
the eastern part of the Nile Delta, widely
exported one of the most famous wines
of antiquity in the late fifth century B.C.
Mende wine could have been stored
in this amphora with its slightly rolled
rounded rim, cylindrical neck, broad
body, and two ovoid handles.

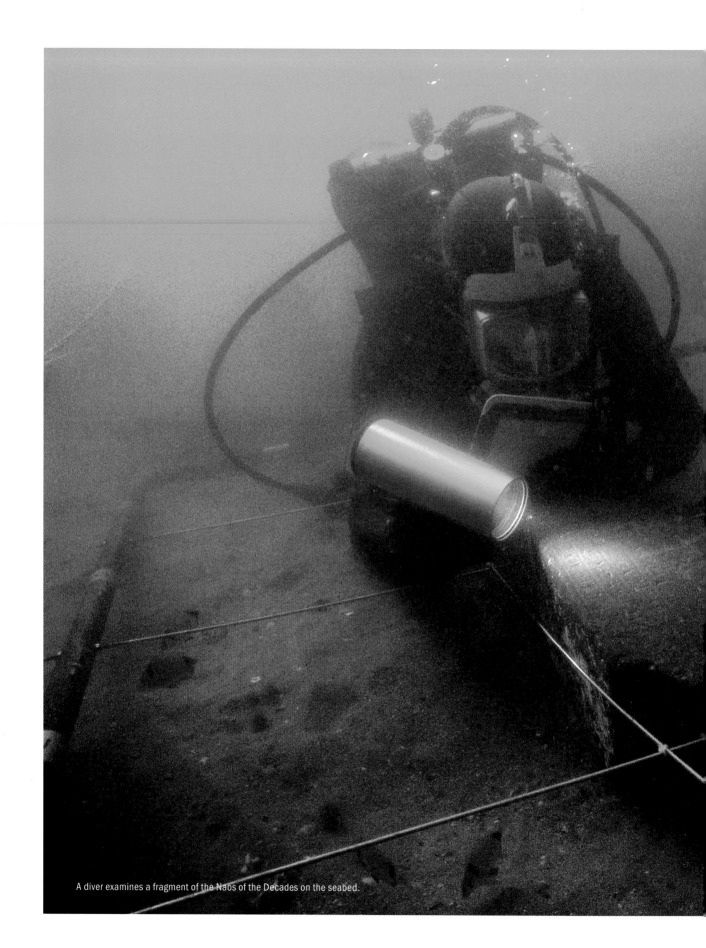
A diver examines a fragment of the Naos of the Decades on the seabed.

Time has eroded the mouth, nose, and eyes of Antonia Minor's exquisite feminine head. The arrangement of hair, parted at the middle of the forehead with two wavy masses flowing down the sides, was characteristic of Antonia Minor. This hairstyle was widely followed in private portraiture, but the size of the sculpture suggests that this was an official portrait, perhaps one commissioned by Antonia herself.

This celebrated Roman woman was born of the political marriage between Mark Antony and Octavia that sealed a pact between Antony and Octavius, Octavia's brother. The marriage gave Mark Antony power over the eastern portion of Roman territory, while Octavian maintained control of the west. Mark Antony had already been involved with Cleopatra at the time Antonia was born. Cleopatra had given birth to twins, Alexander Helios and Cleopatra Selene, whom Mark Antony saw when he visited Cleopatra during Octavia's pregnancy.

At about that time, Mark Antony married Cleopatra in an Egyptian ceremony, though the marriage was never recognized by Rome. Meanwhile, Antonia Minor was born to Octavia in Greece. Mark Antony died before ever meeting this daughter.

■ **Sphinx**

Red granite | Ptolemaic period
H. 46 cm | W. 36 cm | L. 114 cm

Although it is broken at the neck, the back edge and lappets of the nemes headdress on this intact sphinx body remains visible. The midsection of the body is compact, and the ends of the forepaws are curved slightly outward.

■ Bowl

Bronze | Egyptian Late Period
H. 6 cm | Diam. 13.3 cm | Wt. 378 g

The upper part of this bowl is now obscured, and
little can be said with certainty about its original
form. It is possible to surmise that the vessel has
a short neck, which flares outward from the bowl,
and probably no pronounced rim, thus identifiable
as what is generally called a calyx cup.

■ Simpulum

Bronze | 6th–2nd c. B.C.
Left: L. 46.5 cm | Diam. 5.3 cm | Wt. 540 g
Right: L. 48 cm | Diam. 6 cm | Wt. 456 g

These two ladles are completely covered in the remains
of marine organisms and little can be made of their
original features. However, the object does adequately
demonstrate the extent to which conditions in the water can
affect archaeological artifacts. The ladle on the right has a
large square-sectioned handle with a duck's head terminal
and a large bowl.

■ Oil lamp

Lead | 5th–4th c. B.C.
H. 1.3 cm | Diam. 12 cm

This lead oil lamp is circular, and pinched in
at one place on the lip to fashion a handle.
The shape conforms perfectly to the typology
of ceramic oil lamps.

■ Stone with gold fragments

Limestone and gold | 6th–2nd c. B.C.
H. 15 cm | W. 30 cm | L. 30 cm

This limestone receptacle with gold fragments may
have served practical or more luxurious functions.
The majority of gold works found in Heracleion were
discovered around the temple, where offerings of
fine jewelry would have been made to the gods.

Two divers measure a gleaming treasure on the seafloor.

These fragments of a right and left foot on a plinth come from a life-size statue in the Greek style made from stone quarried in Egypt. The left foot is intact from the toes to the edge of the heel; the right foot is intact from the toes to the arch. There has been substantial care given to the anatomy of the foot: The arch is rendered true to nature, and there are individual articulations of the joints of the toes.

Alexandria's urban design, artistic production, and way of life were largely Greek, even under Cleopatra, who was as interested in portraying herself as an authentic Egyptian pharaoh as she was in fostering beneficial relations with the outside world. The naturalistic feel of this piece reflects a shift in Egyptian art that occurred around Cleopatra's time, when artists began prioritizing the accuracy of their representations over the more stylized approaches of the past. One can only imagine the possibilities for who might be depicted in the remainder of this statue, from one of the draped male statues that were so common in ancient Egypt to a royal figure of great importance.

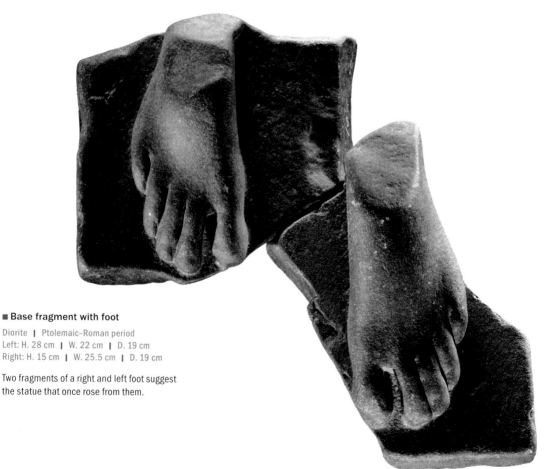

■ **Base fragment with foot**

Diorite | Ptolemaic–Roman period
Left: H. 28 cm | W. 22 cm | D. 19 cm
Right: H. 15 cm | W. 25.5 cm | D. 19 cm

Two fragments of a right and left foot suggest
the statue that once rose from them.

Coin hoard

Bronze | Ptolemaic period

Coins from Canopus and Heracleion bear witness to the political vicissitudes of the two cities, from their origins as important pharaonic trading centers through Alexander the Great's conquest to the fall of Cleopatra.

False beard

Bronze | Egyptian Late Period-Ptolemaic period
L. 16.6 cm | W. 4.6 cm

False beards were often worn, as in ancient Egypt, in imitation of their bearded gods. This bronze false beard is hollow cast, and most likely belonged to a statue of Osiris. The upper part has a trapezoidal protrusion that may have been used for fastening the beard onto the statue.

Sarcophagus topped with a figurine of an ichneumon or a shrew

Bronze | 6th–2nd c. B.C.
H. 3.50 cm | W. 1.70 cm | L. 7 cm

Perched on top of a small bronze sarcophagus is a figurine of either an ichneumon, the sacred mongoose of the Nile, or a shrew. The size of the box is better adapted to the latter rodent, assuming that it contained the entire body of the animal. The mummies of shrews are abundant and care was taken to preserve them in bronze or wooden boxes.

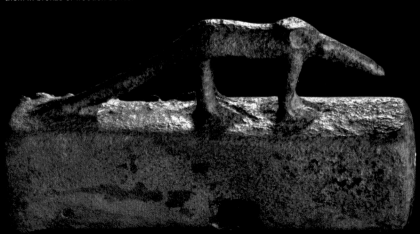

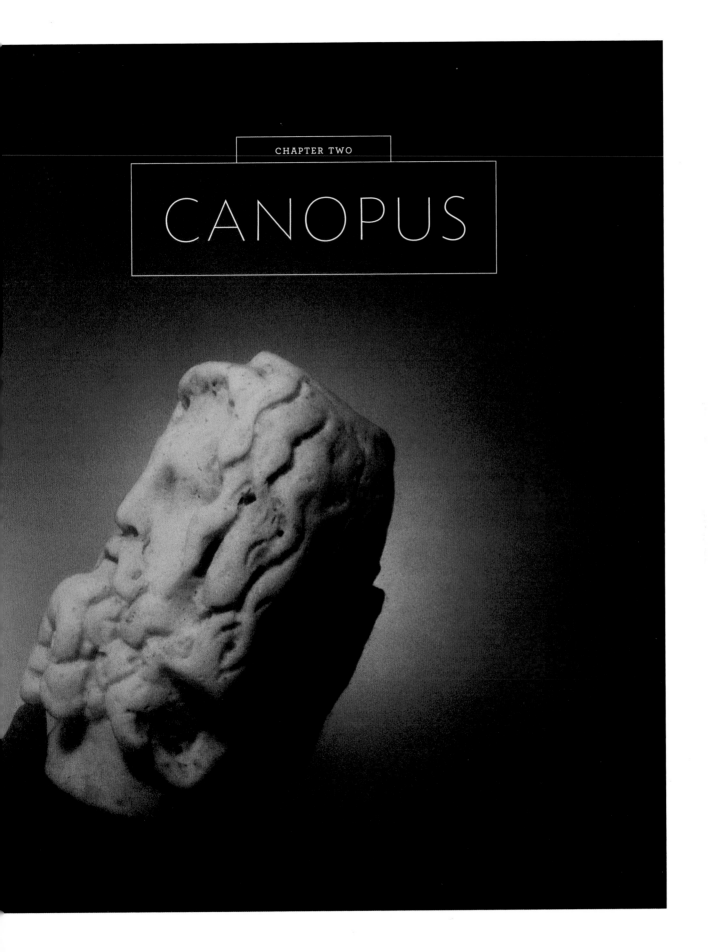

CHAPTER TWO

CANOPUS

CITY DEDICATED to
SERAPIS

Franck Goddio _____

At its peak, ancient Canopus—about 26 kilometers from Alexandria and 1.2 kilometers east of the modern port of Aboukir—was at once the holiest and the most indulgent city in all of Egypt. Masses of people would journey annually to this city during the Ptolemaic period to honor the god Osiris, and later Serapis, his Ptolemaic-era reinterpretation. At the same time, Canopus was the locale for outlandish parties and festivals so spectacular that even the last queen of Egypt couldn't resist.

According to ancient Egyptian myth, Osiris of Canopus was killed by Set, his jealous brother, who trapped him in a sarcophagus and threw it into the Nile. Isis, Osiris's sister, searched until she found her brother's coffin in modern-day Lebanon and brought him home for a proper burial. But Set, determined to destroy all traces of Osiris, dug up his body and dismembered him into 14 pieces, scattering them throughout Egypt. Again, Isis searched high and low for the remains of her brother. Miraculously, she found every piece except one. Using her magical powers, she was able to resurrect her brother and conceive a child by him, whom they named Horus. In the end, Osiris became the god of the afterlife and Isis the goddess of motherhood, fertility, and magic.

A trilingual decree dating from 238 B.C. records that every year, after seeds had sprouted, a divine ship would sail from Heracleion to Canopus in honor of Osiris. Worshippers would construct two effigies, one of vegetables and grains and the other of minerals, statues erected that would represent the resurrected god through the year to come. Believers would conduct a liturgical procession between the two cities, following the paths of the sun and moon, originating in Heracleion to the east and traveling westward toward Canopus.

UNDERWATER DISCOVERIES

Mirroring the historical record, IEASM researchers have discovered a large canal running between these two sunken cities that they believe to be the route taken by this religious procession. The waterway was found to be strewn with dishes used to make offerings, as well as votive ships, bowl lamps, and ladles with handles fashioned into ducks, geese, or other birds. All these objects are presumed to have been used in sacred rites. These religious objects bear witness not only to the importance of the cult of Osiris, but also to the city of Canopus, the center of worship for one of Egypt's most powerful gods.

Prince Omar Toussoun's initial rediscovery of Canopus in 1933 uncovered column shafts, limestone blocks, and other architectural elements. Northwest of this area, recent dives have turned up a temple, very likely the one described in ancient texts as dedicated to Serapis, a composite deity introduced by early Ptolemaic leaders in an effort to unify the Greek and Egyptian religions. In Canopus, the god was given the Greek name Serapis. He combined the characteristics of Egyptian gods (Osiris-Apis) and the Greek (Zeus, Hades, and Dionysus). He was pictured as bearded and enthroned, the god of the dead, the healer god, the god of fertility, and the protector of sailors.

The new temple site found underwater contains over 100 meters of large limestone blocks buried beneath 2 meters of sediment, and may represent the largest temple ever consecrated to Serapis. Divers have excavated a remarkable 4-meter marble head of Serapis from the site, doubtless the principal effigy of him in this temple. Other artifacts recovered nearby, including coins and crosses, confirm that Canopus eventually became a vast Christian settlement as well.

During the first and second centuries A.D., Osiris of Canopus was portrayed in the form of an oval container crowned by a human head, an example of which is the white marble vessel discovered at the site. Such representations of the resurrected god were containers for water from the Nile flood, which was associated with humors, or essential fluids, that emanated from the god's body. These religious objects bear witness to the importance of the cult of Osiris both in Canopus and in the wider Mediterranean world.

According to accounts from Cleopatra's time, the temple of Serapis was greatly venerated by Egyptians and pilgrims, some of whom came from far away to receive the blessings of Serapis. All believed in the temple's power to perform miraculous healings, and crowds gathered for consultations with the oracle. Those seeking healing underwent a process called incubation: In the course of a night spent close to the shrine, the ailing sleeper would have a dream that contained a message about the remedy or therapy needed to result in a cure. These miracles of Serapis were then recorded in the temple archives.

Researchers also found an area meant for unused statuary between the temple of Serapis and the Christian complex. This was likely a sculptural scrap yard where statues were dismantled and their materials reused. Not far away, IEASM researchers discovered several blocks of granite covered with hieroglyphs that they now know come from the famous monolithic chapel referred to as Naos of the Decades, parts of which had already been discovered and held in the Greco-Roman Museum in Alexandria and in the Louvre from as early as 1817.

A *naos* is the inner sanctum of a temple, and this remarkable artifact probably formed an inside wall or partition. Set up by King Nectanebo I in the fourth century B.C. for the benefit of a god worshipped in a town to the east of the Nile Delta, the Naos of the Decades is engraved with a calendar that divides the year into ten-day segments, called decades, timed with the rising of certain stars. Several pieces of this massive wall have been recovered during IEASM dives, and one of them gives an unparalleled account of the story of creation. According to the inscription, the genesis of the sky and stars occurred when the god Shu, personifying the atmosphere, placed himself between sky and earth. Shu set the stars in motion and became the god of the astrological commentaries of each decade, as well as the inflictor of sickness and death upon the enemies of Egypt. The Naos of the Decades, which predates the Ptolemaic period by more than half a century, is of infinite interest for the study of the evolution of ideas.

CLEOPATRA'S CANOPUS

In the Ptolemaic period, masses of people attended the lavish—and often hedonistic—festivals celebrated in the canal connecting Canopus with Alexandria. In the first century A.D., Greek historian and geographer Strabo wrote of the city, saying that Canopus "has a temple of Serapis, the object of great devotion, . . . but there is a crowd of people who go to the public festivals, and come down from Alexandria on the canal; night and day the canal is covered with boats where men and women play the flute and dance wildly." Renowned for its easy way of life, Canopus was the place to which Cleopatra and Mark Antony fled to shelter their affair. Roman propaganda condemned the Canopic lifestyle as one based entirely on pleasure and denounced Cleopatra and Mark Antony as lustful despots. Octavius, Mark Antony's most powerful Roman enemy, insulted his fellow coun-tryman by claiming that he had "become one of the cymbal players from Canopus."

Late in the fourth century A.D., Christians ransacked pagan sanctuaries throughout the Mediterranean, bringing the extravagant Canopic lifestyle to a close. The shrine of Serapis was all but destroyed; according to a contemporary account, "only the foundation was left, because of the weight of the stones, which were not easy to move." Such destruction meant that any idols inside were destroyed. Christians built a massive monastery near the temple ruins, as well as a martyrium holding the remains of St. Cyrus and of St. John, two martyrs said to have inherited the prophetic and healing powers once embodied by Serapis. Christian pilgrims came to the place to pray or be healed, much as the ailing Egyptians had for centuries before.

"The entry of Osiris in the holy barque takes place here yearly at the defined time, at the temple at [Heracleion] . . . and the inhabitants of temples of first rank throughout make burnt offerings on the altars of the temples of the first rank, right and left."

— THE CANOPUS DECREE (circa 239 B.C.)

Of this Christian worship center, IEASM's research team has uncovered a large square building, 30 meters long and up to 3 meters tall, as well as other smaller buildings to the west of the temple of Serapis. The archaeological material recovered from these excavations—jewels, crosses, coins, and seals, all from the Byzantine era—confirm that this area became a vast Christian settlement in the centuries after Cleopatra's suicide brought the Ptolemaic era to a close. Layers of history characterize the underwater ruins of Canopus, a city that will always be defined by its importance in Egyptian religion and by its notoriety as a place of indulgence and pleasure and a sanctuary for the equally notorious Cleopatra. ∎

PAGES 58-59: A diver admires a marble head of the god Serapis from Egypt's Roman period.

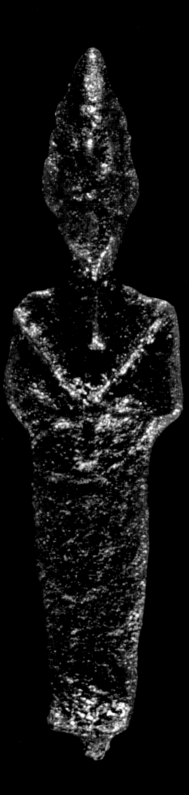

■ Statuette of Osiris

Bronze | Egyptian Late Period–Ptolemaic period
H. 9.1 cm | W. 2.2 cm | D. 1 cm

The god Osiris was honored at Canopus
during the month of Khoiak, around December.
The many figurines of him that have been found
there are likely votive offerings.

■ Statuette of Isis

Bronze | Egyptian Late Period–Ptolemaic period
H. 18 cm | W. 4.1 cm | D. 1.8 cm

The Hathoric crown that adorns the head of the
goddess Isis is composed of two horns wrapped
around a lunar disk. Here, Isis is depicted nursing
her son Harpocrates, known to the Egyptians as
Horus. The nude child bears the forelock of youth.

Statuette of Harpocrates

Bronze | Egyptian Late Period–Ptolemaic period
H. 9.2 cm | W. 2.7 cm | D. 1.3 cm

Traditionally portrayed with the forelock of
youth, Harpocrates (left), son of Isis and Osiris,
sometimes wears the double crown of Upper
and Lower Egypt. He can be shown nude and
seated, holding his arms at his sides or lifting
his finger to his mouth.

Statuette of Osiris

Bronze | Egyptian Late Period–Ptolemaic period
H. 21 cm | W. 4.3 cm | D. 2.2 cm

Osiris was often depicted with a false beard
and the atef crown. Here, he wears a collar
and carries the traditional scepter and flail.
Hieroglyphs line the base of the statue and
the face, on which Osiris's name is legible.

Wearing the traditional head covering of the ancient pharaohs, called the nemes, the head of this pharaoh has highly detailed, well-preserved workmanship. A simple piece of fabric that folded behind the ears and twisted at the nape of the neck, the nemes was a fundamental part of the pharaoh's dress. The head of this pharaoh is protected by a uraeus, a cobra that bestowed the power of the gods upon the ruler. The false beard is broken beneath the receding chin, and the almond-shaped eyes of the royal effigy have lost their inlays.

The smooth, supple, and precise sculpting of the face is characteristic of the Saite Renaissance, a movement that occurred during the 26th dynasty (664–525 B.C.), when art flourished and artists became inspired to interpret traditional styles in a more naturalistic light. This dynasty of native Egyptian kings was the last to rule before the Persian conquest in 525 B.C., marking the beginning of the Egyptian Late Period. Under the Saite kings, Egypt experienced a period of increased prosperity, and the greatness of Egypt was reestablished after a period of decline and foreign rule. In many ways, this prosperity was similar to the way Egypt flourished during Cleopatra's rule, despite the looming threat of Rome's invasion.

Head of a pharaoh

Diorite | Saite dynasty (26th dynasty)
H. 35 cm | W. 30 cm | D. 29 cm

This pharaoh's head displays the traditional
head covering of Egyptian pharaohs.

Simpula

Bronze | Ptolemaic period
L. 26.5-56.8 cm | Diam. 4.1-6.1 cm | Wt. 92 g

The long, straight, flat handles of these ladles
end in the curved head of a duck. Typical of
instruments used for ceremonies or in everyday
life during the Ptolemaic period, the bowls
are wide and rather shallow, with some holes
caused by corrosion.

■ Strainer

Ptolemaic period
Bronze ┃ 6th–2nd c. B.C.
H. 2.7 cm ┃ L. 22 cm ┃ Diam. (ext.) 9.1 cm
Diam. (filter) 4.6 cm ┃ Th. 0.1 cm

Beautifully crafted bronze wine strainers such as
this one may have been used in the lavish parties
around the time of Cleopatra. The handle ends in
the curved head of a goose, and two fine elongated
elements on the side opposite the handle indicate
that this particular piece could be hung from a wall
or propped against another container.

■ Simpulum

Bronze ┃ 6th–2nd c. B.C.
L. 52.2 cm ┃ Diam. 6.7 cm ┃ Wt. 505 g

Still intact, this ladle has a relatively deep
semi-ovoid bowl with a flat rim. The long
handle becomes larger toward the bowl,
and its square cross section ends in a
hooked fowl head.

■ Large bronze brazier

Bronze ┃ 4th c. B.C.
H. 23 cm ┃ Diam. 46 cm

The little that is known of Egyptian housing during
the Greco-Roman period shows that there was not
necessarily a specific area or room dedicated to food
preparation. Braziers such as this one had handles so
that they could be carried to any part of the house.

The shape of this Ptolemaic offering table (opposite) is similar to the ancient Egyptian hieroglyph that meant *hetep,* "offering" —a loaf of bread on a mat. It suggests that an offering may have rested upon the table, ready to be consumed by the gods. The top is surrounded by a trough, which nearly divides the central area of the stone into two halves but terminates at the front in a U-shaped symbol. Perhaps this particular offering table was left unfinished by its creator. Two cartouche-shaped impressions in the stone provided a place where physical offerings could be deposited for the god.

The city of Canopus was, above all, a spiritual place. Egyptian temples, like the important temple to Serapis, usually contained offering tables. People would come from far and wide to this temple in hopes that Serapis might cure them of their ailments.

Many offerings were brought to the god so that he would be satisfied and want to help the visitor in question. The objects sacrificed varied widely, but they may have included bread, beer, linen, fowl, meat, alabaster, oil, papyrus, or even flowers. The offering tables provided a symbolic and a physical location for commodities intended for the god's consumption.

■ **Brazier**

Bronze | 4th–2nd c. B.C.
H. 7.8 cm | Diam. 7.4–8.6 cm | Wt. 413 g

With its crenellated top, this brazier almost evokes an ancient fortification. It is perfectly proportioned to hold a wide circular spoon found nearby in the waters of Heracleion.

A diver marvels at a large fragment of a stela found in the underwater city of Heracleion.

■ Mirror

Bronze | 6th–2nd c. B.C.
H. 19.8 cm | Diam. 15 cm | Th. 0.6 cm | Wt. 703 g

Given its wide, circular impressions, one or both
sides of this artifact were likely reflective, though
the sediment encrusted around the object prevents
closer examination.

■ Miniature mirror

Lead | Roman period
H. 2.5 cm | Diam. 4.4 cm | Th. 0.3 cm

Exquisite decorations adorning the surface of this
mirror suggest that this item may have been used by a
person of high stature in Egyptian society. Alternatively,
this mirror may have been a votive offering, meant for
the use of one of the gods.

Head of Serapis

Marble | 2nd c. B.C.
H. 59 cm | W. 34 cm | D. 34 cm

The eroded head of Serapis depicts
an important deity for Greeks and
Egyptians alike.

Divers uncovered this isolated head of Serapis at a distance from a group of sculptures found lying in a Canopic dumping ground. Life-size but badly eroded, the white marble is broken horizontally at the base of the neck. Serapis's face is elongated, the nose short, and the eyes deep-set. A mustache with curled and drooping ends surmounts the carefully modeled mouth, and the god's abundant beard hangs in well-separated curls. The treatment of the hair and comparative study of similar marble statues make it possible to date this head of Serapis to around the second century B.C.

The flattened surface at the top of the head is designed for attaching the calathos, the traditional crown worn by this divinity. The calathos, which held grains and other foods, was often decorated with an olive branch on statues such as this one.

Sometimes the calathos crown was replaced by the atef crown generally worn by the god Osiris, a major influence on the hybrid god Serapis. Like Osiris, Serapis was said to ensure the fertility of the land so that agriculture could prosper. At times he was also referred to as the god of the afterlife.

■ **Erotic statuette**

Limestone | Ptolemaic period
H. 14 cm | W. 5 cm

Sculptors oversimplified the features of so-called erotica figurines, many of which were unearthed on the sites of several temples dating back to the Ptolemaic period. The lower part of this statuette is broken below the woman's pubis.

Incense burner

Bronze | 6th–2nd c. B.C.
H. 21.4 cm | H. (foot) 18.8 cm
Diam. (foot) 3.2-3.8 cm | Diam. (dish) 9.5 cm

The two components of this incense burner
are its hollow circular foot and its circular dish.
The stand mimics the widening shape of a palm
tree; the dish held incense used in rituals and
processions of Canopus.

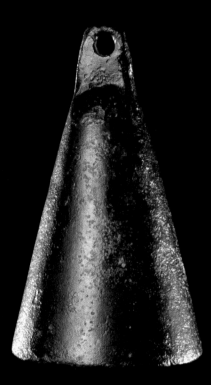

Bells

Bronze | 6th–2nd c. B.C.
Left: H. 7.5 cm | Diam. 5.2 cm | Th. 0.2 cm
Right: H. 7.6 cm | Diam. 4.5–5.2 cm
Th. 0.4 cm | Wt. 143 g

Bells with a conical profile and an oval cup may
have been used in the festivals and rituals of
Canopus. The rectangular ring, made from the
same plate of metal, enabled these bells to be
hung on a wall.

Console or table leg

Granodiorite | Ptolemaic period
H. 70 cm | W. 21 cm

Part of a console or table leg, this object was
crafted in the form of a large animal's hind leg,
perhaps the sacred bull. Given the spiritual ele-
ment to the artifact, and the fact that it was
discovered in Canopus, scientists believe that
this console may have been an offering by the
Ptolemies to furnish the holy sanctuary of Serapis.

Hook

Bronze | 6th–2nd c. B.C.
L. 9.5 cm | Diam. 4.3 cm | Th. 1.2 cm

The curved head of a duck emerging from this
circular ring was not the only one of its kind. In fact,
the duck was a frequent motif, both in mural painting and in tomb reliefs. This motif of a curved duck
head is particularly well represented in Heracleion
in the numerous simpula discovered at the site.

Incense burner

Bronze | 6th–2nd c. B.C.
H. 7.9 cm | Diam. 10.4 cm | Wt. 668 g

The round bowl of this incense burner rests on
three legs formed like cloven hooves to resemble
those of a cow. Incense, an expensive commodity
in ancient Egypt, was believed to possess purifying
qualities. The rite of offering incense purified the
air of all evil and brought the officiant and
the beneficiary into the sacred realm.

Thousands of years have come and gone since this bull-shaped table leg adorned the Serapeum.

■ Basin

Bronze | 4th–2nd c. B.C.
H. 13.3 cm | Diam. 25.8 cm

Jewelry aside, the metal finds from Heracleion are almost exclusively bronze and lead. This basin is an example of the many metal vessels found at the site.

■ Basin

Bronze | 4th–2nd c. B.C.
H. 17 cm | Diam. 25.3 cm | Th. 0.3 cm
Wt. 111.6 g

Some small corrosion holes are visible in this basin, though its shape recalls the basins with smaller dimensions discovered in the fourth to second centuries B.C.

■ Receptacle

Bronze | Ptolemaic period
H. 5.6 cm | Diam. 10.2 cm | Th. 0.2 cm
Wt. 241 g

The bowing sides of the small pot show the effects of many years underwater. The hole in the center of the base plate suggests that the container was once attached to some larger object and may have been used to offer or burn incense.

Basin

Bronze | 6th–2nd c. B.C.
H. 11.9 cm | Diam. 42.1 cm

This basin has a flared rim and almost
vertical sides that taper out slightly toward
the top. A darkened area on the bottom
surface of the base could possibly be a sign
of heating.

Cup

Bronze | Ptolemaic period
H. 7 cm | Diam. 12.2 cm

Almost entirely corroded, a green patina
covers almost all surfaces of this cup.
The exterior of the bowl is simple, absent of
decoration except for an incised line near
the flat edge. The remains of two handles
appear now as two small cylinders, to which
a movable handle was probably attached.

■ Sistrum and arched frame

Bronze | 6th–2nd c. B.C.
H. 14 cm | W. 4 cm | Th. 1.2 cm | Wt. 107 g

The sistrum is one of the principal bronze musical instruments found at Canopus. A rattle equipped with bars arranged in parallel tiers in a frame, the instrument had a metallic sound. Its decorated handle almost always ends in the head of Hathor, a goddess sometimes conflated with Isis.

■ Lamp

Bronze | Ptolemaic period
Bottom: H. 11 cm | W. 7.6 cm | L. 13.2 cm
Top: L. 36.4 cm | W. 1.1 cm

Most lamps discovered at Heracleion are simple oil dishes, but this one has an long, egg-shaped body, hoofed feet, and a duck-shaped handle. Used in cult ceremonies for Isis, lamps illuminated temple chapels or held offerings to the gods.

■ Tongs

Bronze | 6th–2nd c. B.C.
L. 45.9 cm | Th. 0.4 cm | Wt. 240 g

Bronze tongs ending in two outstretched hands may have been used to handle burning coals.

■ Nails

Bronze | 6th–2nd c. B.C.
L. 20–25 cm

Evidence of daily craftsmanship in
Canopus, bronze nails in different
shapes and length were discovered at
the site.

■ Handles

Bronze | 6th–2nd c. B.C.

These two handles, found together,
come from two different objects, as
indicated by their different sizes.

The head of Serapis lies on the ocean floor, far removed from the temple where it might have once stood.

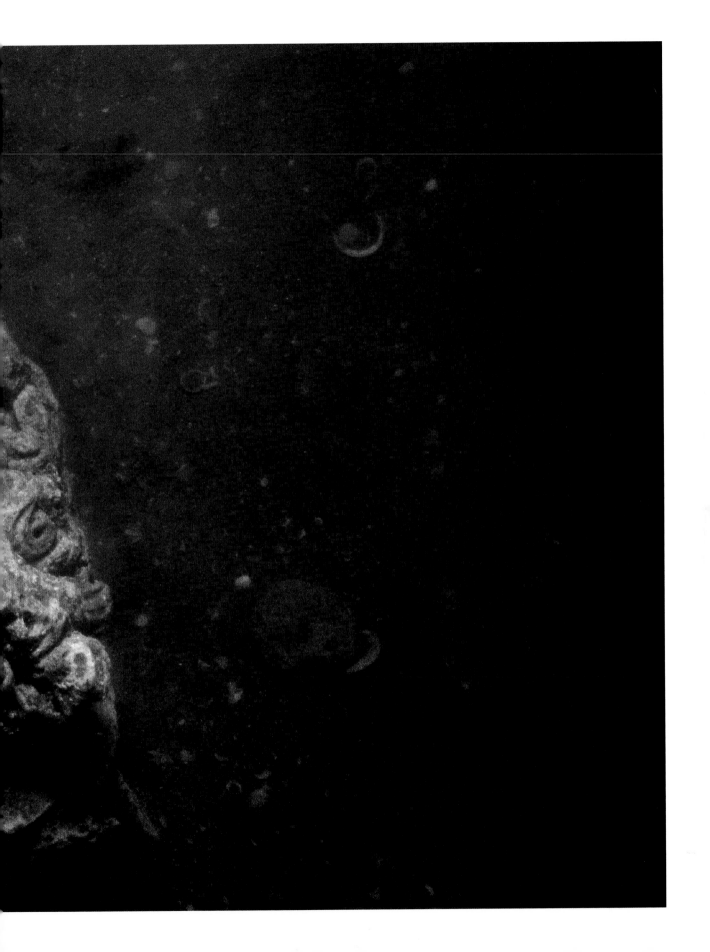

Naos of the Decades

Granodiorite | 30th dynasty,
Nectanebo I (380–362 B.C.)
H. 178 cm | W. 80 cm | L. 88 cm

The structure of this naos, or niche
for temple statues, forms a monument
to the god Shu.

The type of shrine known as a naos was a niche made to hold the statue of a deity set up in the rear of a temple, the holiest part. This naos, erected by Pharaoh Nectanebo I (380-362 B.C.), has been shattered into many pieces, probably during the destruction of the Canopic temples by the Christians. Some surfaces have been considerably abraded by time spent in the water. This remarkable naos, known as the Naos of the Decades, was discovered in the Bay of Aboukir. Parts of it were already in the Louvre in Paris, but the research team excavated the remaining pieces.

This naos is dedicated to the god Shu, who personified the gaseous atmosphere that Egyptians believed to exist between sky and earth. The inside of the naos contained a golden figure of Shu in the form of a lion, which shone brilliantly against the dark walls of the naos like a bright sun against the backdrop of night.

Perhaps the naos's most remarkable feature is the chiseled calendar that divides the Egyptian year into ten-day periods called decades. The first known to do so, the framed decade fields are distributed on the left, right, and rear facades of the chapel and arranged in three registers on each side. There are 36 large, vertical fields, denoting the 36 decades of the year. A 37th field is inserted for the five days that the Egyptians added to the year in order to complete the 365-day year. The complexity of this calendar underscores the advanced innovation of ancient Egyptian society.

The reverse of the Naos of the Decades, inscribed with hieroglyphics, represents Egypt's calendar.

Lekythos

Bronze | Egyptian Late Period–Ptolemaic period
H. 20.9 cm | Diam. 3.8–8.1 cm
Th. 0.1 cm | Wt. 614 g

A typical classical squat lekythos, the small opening
at the top of this vessel prevented the precious oils
inside from spilling out. The smooth curve of the neck
blends into the globular body. The handle, decorated
with four indented lines, was created from the same
piece of metal as the rim.

■ Tumbler and beaker

Bronze | Ptolemaic period
Tumbler: H. 13 cm | Diam. 9.7 cm | Th. 0.2 cm
Beaker: H. 14.5 cm | Diam. 11 cm

This cylindrical tumbler and beaker have high bodies. The neck is only slightly turned in, and the thicker bottom is slightly rounded. One can envision Cleopatra pouring herself a drink or performing experiments with vessels such as these.

■ Bowl with handle

Bronze | Ptolemaic period
H. 9.6 cm | Diam. 25.2 cm | Th. 0.2 cm | Wt. 535 g

Deep bowls with handles seem to have appeared in metalware around the second half of the fourth century B.C. They were probably used during dining as containers for food or liquid.

■ Bowl

Bronze | 5th–2nd c. B.C.
H. 6.9 cm | Diam. 13.1 cm | Th. 0.2 cm

Archaeologists uncovered several similar vessels in Heracleion. These were practical bowls, with a distinctive ridge marking a break in the profile between a convex belly and a straight or slightly concave upper part.

A Ptolemaic bronze bowl discovered in an excavation lies among seashells.

Cup

Bronze | 6th–4th c. B.C.
H. 8.5 cm | Diam. 9.6 cm | Th. 0.1 cm | Wt. 230 g

A simple rosette design found on pots throughout the Hellenistic world adorns the central underbelly of this cup. Because more vessels of this style have been found in Egypt than anywhere else, some believe that this decorative style was manufactured in Alexandria and then widely exported.

Situla with Greek inscription

Bronze | Ptolemaic period
H. 25 cm | Diam. (neck) 26.8 cm
Diam. (base) 28.5 cm | Th. 0.4 cm

The Greek inscription on the handle of this situla, or bucket, is no longer legible. In Egyptian religion, situlae were used for cult libations and were often donated by individuals.

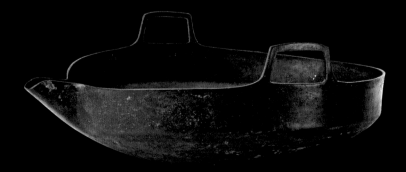

Receptacle with spout

Bronze | 5th–2nd c. B.C.
H. 13 cm | Diam. 41.5 cm | Th. 0.3 cm | Wt. 3.869 g

The hemispherical body, narrow triangular spout, and dual handles welded to the edge of the container suggest that this shallow receptacle was once used for pouring an unknown liquid.

■ Bowl

Bronze | 5th–2nd c. B.C.
H. 7.2 cm | Diam. 11.2 cm | Th. 0.1 cm

The lip of this vessel has been drawn outward and then pulled down to create a slight overhang. The inclusion of this rim makes it unlikely that the vessel was ever used for drinking.

■ Bowl

Bronze | 5th–2nd c. B.C.
H. 6.4 cm | Diam. 10.5 cm
Th. 0.35 cm | Wt. 294 g

With straight, diverging sides and a rounded underbelly, this bowl probably lent itself to practical uses, perhaps in a common household in Canopus. An incised line runs around the circumference approximately half a centimeter below the square-topped rim.

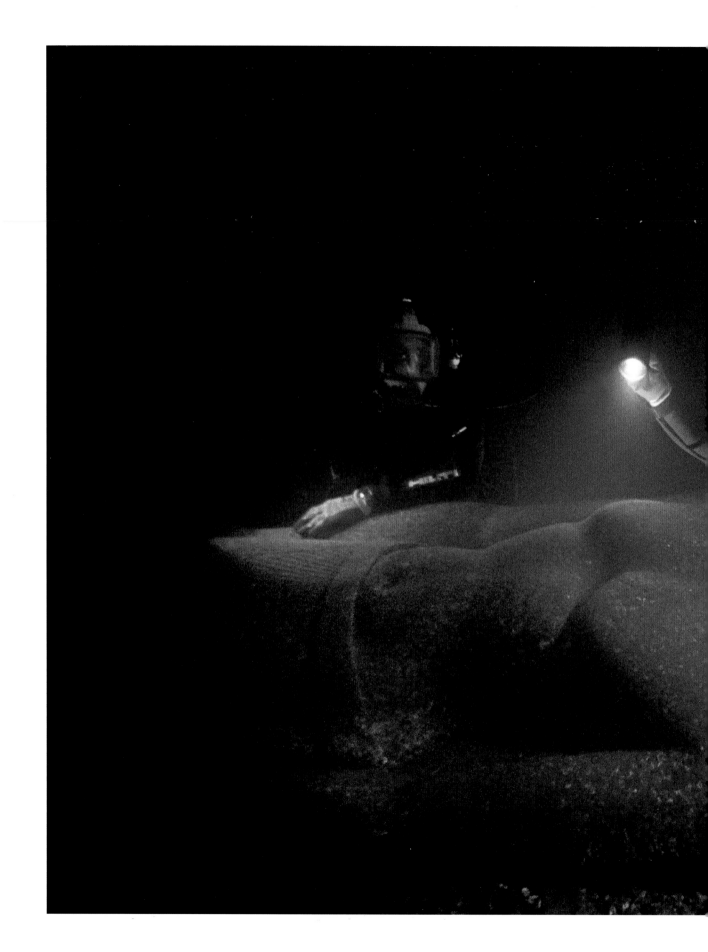

CHAPTER THREE

HERACLEION

GATEWAY into EGYPT'S
NILE DELTA

Franck Goddio

Situated northeast of Alexandria, the relatively shallow waters of the Bay of Aboukir spread over a considerable area. Beneath these waters lie monuments of a world we have only read about. Abundant literary, epigraphic, and papyrological documentation, together with the testimonies of early explorers and archaeological information provided by Egypt's Supreme Council of Antiquities (SCA), all indicated that we had much to expect from this region. Canopus, Thonis, Heracleion—for centuries the names of these cities, passed down to us by ancient writers, have inspired visions of splendor—but archaeologists had not located them.

In fact, when IEASM researchers discovered a submerged expanse of ruins 6 kilometers from the Bay of Aboukir, they found it nearly impossible to connect the ruins with buildings and settlements described by ancient writers. Divers found a 150-meter wall stretching around a temple, for example, but the deity worshipped in the temple, and the name of the settlement surrounding the temple, remained a mystery.

Eventually scientists recognized that they had found a monument of the utmost significance to the history of the Ptolemies. It was the temple of Heracleion, named after the Greek god Heracles, the sacred location where each new pharaoh was crowned. The research team had discovered the ancient city of Heracleion, a city that once served as the primary commercial entrance into Egypt and drew pilgrims from throughout the Mediterranean to worship at its temple. Cleopatra herself might have received the inventory of her earthly and celestial kingdom here, little knowing that she would be the last of her dynasty to rule over her homeland.

The main god worshipped in the temple was Amon-Gereb, whose blessing was believed necessary to confirm each new pharaoh's power. The Ptolemaic kings claimed to be descendants of Heracles, son of Zeus, on the paternal side, and of Dionysus, son of Zeus, on the maternal side. Thus they found great benefit in showering Heracles with gifts in his temple, and investigation of the temple site now underwater reveals evidence of such activities.

MONUMENTAL MONARCHS

Among the remarkable objects found in the vicinity are two towering pink granite figures representing a Ptolemaic king and his wife, the most majestic of all the statuary recovered from Heracleion. These statues have much to tell us about Ptolemaic royalty. Found in five separate pieces and measuring 5 meters tall, the king is practically complete. His arms fall alongside his body. His right fist holds the enigmatic small cylinder found in the hands of other sculptures of important men of Egypt. His dress is simple and classic: Bare-chested, the king wears the traditional shendjyt kilt, or loincloth. On his head he wears the pschent, or double crown expressing the unification of Upper and Lower Egypt, adorned on the front with a uraeus, a cobra that symbolized divine power in ancient Egypt, whose body is schematized in the shape of two lateral rings.

In the companion sculpture, the queen wears a classical tripartite wig with minutely detailed braids. Her body is molded in the usual, finely pleated dress, which ends just above the ankles. Her Hathoric crown, worn traditionally by royal wives, includes cow horns, a sun disk, and feathers. A uraeus rising from her forehead also signals her royalty.

Since the Ptolemaic kings were originally of Macedonian descent, they chose to portray themselves through statues such as these, which borrowed many elements from the Egyptian pharaonic traditions and helped to solidify their authenticity as rulers. The Ptolemies wanted to be seen as the natural successors to the ancient pharaohs in order to set themselves apart from the similarly foreign but widely disdained Persian rulers who had recently conquered Egypt. They attempted to ensure their power by incorporating themselves into the spiritual rituals of the time, and they often depicted themselves as incarnations of Heracles, merging their political power with the spiritual power of the gods.

MINGLING OF THE GODS

Greek and Egyptian interpretations conflated the god Amun with Zeus, Amun's consort Mut with the Greek Hera, and Khonsu with Heracles. These amalgamations allowed the Greeks to view Khonsu as an image of Heracles, who, according to ancient myth, had once stopped over in this part of the Nile Delta. Khonsu was one of the childlike guises that all the Egyptian god-sons assumed. Figurines from the Roman era show him armed like the famous statue of Heracles, reinforcing the assimilation of the two deities. In most depictions, the divine child wears a complex head ornament called a hem-hem crown: three bundles of reeds, each crowned with a sun, resting on curved rams' horns and flanked on either side by an ostrich feather and the uraeus. Ptolemaic rulers chose to associate themselves with Heracles, also called a divine child, in order to suggest that they, too, were actually the divine children of the gods. In searching the underwater remains of Heracleion, divers found evidence of this fusion of Egyptian and Greek deities, which allowed both peoples religious autonomy and unity with the wider Mediterranean.

> "*For she was a woman of surpassing beauty, and at that time, when she was in the prime of her youth, she was most striking; she also possessed a most charming voice and a knowledge of how to make herself agreeable to every one.*"
>
> — CLEOPATRA, from Cassius Dio, *Roman History* (A.D. 200)

Cleopatra took the assimilation of royalty and spirituality to new heights by comparing herself to the goddess Isis, the model mother and wife. When Cleopatra first visited Mark Antony in the city of Tarsus (in modern-day Turkey), she donned the guise of Aphrodite to win his affection, signaling her divine power. Once Mark Antony became her lover, he quickly became associated with Dionysus and Osiris. The partnership became a royal version of the partnership between Isis and Osiris for the Egyptians, or Aphrodite and Dionysus for the Greeks—the archetypal divine couple, revered by all under their domain. Although the associations began at their first meeting, they endured far longer and continue as part of their legacy.

Most statues discovered in underwater Heracleion date from the Ptolemaic period, but explorations are revealing a long and complicated history of religious practices in the region. While the majority of artifacts date from between the fourth and second centuries B.C., ritual instruments like the magnificent incense burner in the form of a Greek sphinx, bronze models of gods, and vases of alabaster, limestone, and granite date as far back as the sixth century B.C. Utensils and statuettes of gods excavated from the temple are but a few of the objects used in religious activity within the walls of these sanctuaries.

Rich ritual warehouses and cult instruments were also found in the canal that linked the harbors and the lake to the west, by which ships could cross from Heracleion to Canopus.

These objects demonstrate the sacred character of this great body of water, which was utilized in particular in ceremonies honoring Osiris celebrated at both sites and by means of processions between them.

TRADING CENTER

Because of Heracleion's strategic location on the coast, the city had become the primary commercial entrance into Egypt for the wider Mediterranean world prior to the foundation of the city and harbor of Alexandria in 331 B.C. The buildings discovered in Heracleion fit in remarkably with the shape of the local landscape. In the southern part of the city stood the pharaonic temple and surrounding wall, perched on a promontory overlooking the city. A shimmering lake bordered Heracleion to the west and an outer harbor and docks opened onto the Nile to the east. Between them ran a narrow channel through which ships could travel between Heracleion and Canopus. A sandbar protected the harbor, shielding Heracleion from the prevailing northwesterly winds and from storms coming from the northeast.

Between the seventh and fourth centuries B.C., this city connected to the Canopic branch of the Nile and became a thoroughfare of trade with regions of Greece and a control point for foreign ships on their way to the Greek trading post of Naukratis. Ceramics and other artifacts, as well as the remains of vessels and anchors found scattered in the waters of Heracleion, confirm this city's prowess as a site of active trade between Egypt and the lands of the eastern Mediterranean. Alexandria may have trumped Heracleion-Thonis as a commercial port during the Ptolemaic period, but this older city was a religious center that would have influenced and inspired the Egyptian queen. ∎

PAGES 96-97: Dwarfed in its presence, two divers observe the colossus of a Ptolemaic king.

The colossal Ptolemaic king and queen, statue of the god Hapy, and stela of Ptolemy VIII Euergetes II rest together aboard the deck of a research ship.

■ Coin hoard

Silver and bronze | Ptolemaic period

These coins, preserved over thousands of years in the waters of Heracleion, were discovered by Franck Goddio and his research team.

■ Slingshot bullets

Lead | 5th–4th c. B.C.
L. 3–4 cm | W. 2–3 cm

The Egyptian army used projectile weapons with lead ammunition to weaken their enemy before striking with their infantry.

■ Votive boat

Lead | Ptolemaic period
Left: L. 44.5 cm | W. 3.7 cm
Middle: H. 6.2 cm | W. 3.3 cm | L. 37.3 cm
Right: L. 21.5 cm | W. 3 cm

The rudimentary appearance of these lead votive boats results from the loss of the figurines that formerly stood on the deck. A throne sits in the center of each boat, ready to receive royalty. These models evoke the annual procession from Canopus to Heracleion during which the people of Egypt would pay homage to their god Osiris.

■ Votive boat

Lead | Ptolemaic period
L. 12.1 cm | W. 1.6 cm

River-based imagery was central to Egyptian religion. The gods traveled through the sky seated in papyrus skiffs, and on earth the shrines containing their cult images were carried in elaborate sacred boats, this boat being a more rudimentary example.

205 *Hem-hem* crown of Khonsu

Bronze | Egyptian Late Period–Ptolemaic period
H. 15 cm | W. 10 cm

This crown is in the form for the warrior god
Horus of Edfu. A similar crown is sometimes
encountered on the heads of statues of kings.
In the Greco-Roman period, the young Horus,
Harpocrates, was often represented wearing
this headdress as well.

This great queen in red granite (opposite), by far the best preserved of the large pharaonic-style images that we have of the Ptolemaic rulers, was found broken into three fragments whose edges fitted one another. The disappearance of the left knee was likely caused by accidental breakage, and her right shoulder and arm are completely missing. The traditional Hathoric crown worn by royal wives was made separately, but it fits perfectly into the mortise dug into the middle of the skull.

It is impossible to identify which queen the statue represents. The style of the statue has puzzled archaeologists: Although clearly from the Ptolemaic period, it exhibits very few features of Ptolemaic art. Only a few details—such as a single frontal uraeus instead of two—and some delicate touches in the sculpting evoke the Ptolemaic style. This colossus and that of the Ptolemaic king (following page) are imitations of Ramesside models and borrow no details or signs from Hellenic iconography. The knotted scarf and folds of the dress are very different from their depiction in other statues of Ptolemaic queens, making this queen important for research on Ptolemaic iconography and deification. The Ptolemies sought to align themselves with native Egyptian rulers of the past, and so the sculptor of these statues may have co-opted the Ramesside style in a statement of the Ptolemies' authenticity as rulers.

■ **Incense burner**

Limestone | 6th c. B.C.
H. 24.2 cm | W. 9 cm | D. 12 cm
Diam (bowl) 13.5 cm

Precious evidence of the Greek presence at Heracleion, an intact limestone incense burner recalls images of rites and processions in this highly spiritual city. The object below the shallow round bowl is a Greek-style female sphinx, the mark of Greek influence, and perhaps even the mark of Greek workmanship.

Colossus of a Ptolemaic queen

Red granite | Ptolemaic period
H. 490 cm | W. 120 cm | D. 75 cm

The Ptolemaic queen stands tall, a symbol of the female leaders that reigned during this dynasty.

A diver spots the colossal head of a pharaoh during its excavation and cleaning.

■ Ax blade

Bronze | 6th–4th c. B.C.
Left: H. 2.9 cm | W. 6.8 cm
Right: H. 2.9 cm | W. 9.9 cm

Like the dagger, the ax was not a weapon
used by Greek and Egyptian armies. Instead,
they were tools carried on campaign, either by the
pack animals or wagons accompanying the army.

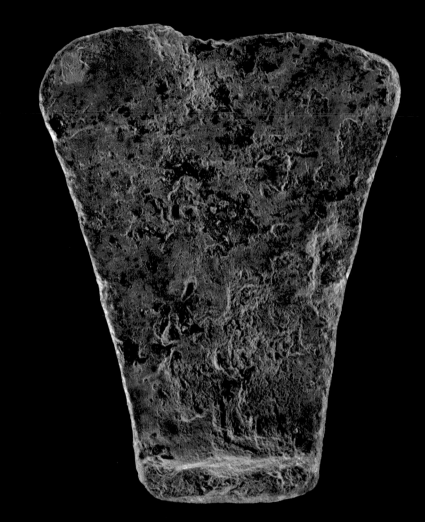

■ Fish hook

Bronze | 6th–2nd c. B.C.
Top left: L. 2.4 cm | Th. 0.2 cm
Top middle: L. 5.9 cm | Th. 0.3 cm
Top right: L. 1.9 cm | W. 2.9 cm | Th. 0.2 cm
Bottom: L. 12 cm | Th. 0.35 cm

Numerous fish hooks with fine barbs have been
discovered at Heracleion. Though fundamentally
practical, these tools testify to the maritime culture
that prevailed in ancient Egypt.

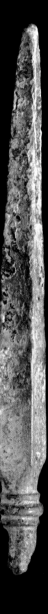

■ Spearhead

Bronze | 6th–4th c. B.C.
L. 18 cm | W. 3 cm

Leaf-shaped spearheads were typical for Greek hoplite spears, which were carried by Greek infantry men and perhaps exported to Egypt. Although iron was more popular and cheapest to produce, bronze spearheads were also made. The rest of this weapon consists of a cylindrical tube into which the wooden shaft was fixed.

■ Spear butt

Bronze | 5th–4th c. B.C.
L. 13.3 cm
L. 35 cm | W.2.5 cm | Diam. 2.5 cm
L. 27 cm | W. 2.5 cm | Diam. 2.5 cm

The spear butt, called a "lizard killer" in ancient Greek, allowed a spear to be planted upright in the ground when not in use. Homer's *Iliad* describes the sleeping comrades of Diomedes, heads resting on their shields, with spears upright beside them, the butt spikes driven deep into the ground.

Researchers hoist the immense body of a Ptolemaic king out of the water in Heracleion.

Colossus of a Ptolemaic king

Red granite | Ptolemaic period
H. 500 cm | W. 150 cm | D. 75 cm | Wt. 5.5 t

Measuring nearly 5 meters tall and found in five separate pieces in Heracleion's underwater ruins, this magnificent Ptolemaic king wears a double crown signifying the unification of Upper and Lower Egypt under the pharaoh. Containing stylistic features from the Ramesside period as well as the 26th dynasty, this king is an incredible example of sculpture during the Ptolemaic period.

Circling the naos in awe, two divers examine their discovery.

Discovered not far from the great temple of Amun, called the Heracleion, this small monolithic red granite chapel may come from the inner sanctum of the temple of Khonsu. Relatively simple in its style, this naos contrasts with the intricate inscriptions and calendar found on the Naos of the Decades from Canopus. Absent of any traces of inscriptions, a circular hole on the right side interrupts the smooth stone surfaces of the naos. The hole was likely made long after the Ptolemaic period in order to repurpose this structure as a watering trough, certainly a more practical function than it had served before.

The first Greeks who settled in Egypt conflated Amun-Re, king of the Egyptian gods, with Zeus, king of the Olympian gods. Moreover, they identified the young lunar god Khonsu, son of Amun of Thebes, with Heracles, son of Zeus, and even located certain stages and minor exploits of the famous itinerant hero on the delta coast. From the tenth century B.C. on, Khonsu had become very popular as a savior god with prophetic healing powers. This would no doubt explain why, in the city of Heracleion, his cult overshadowed that of Amun to the point that foreigners there even considered Amun's temple a "Heracleion," a shrine to Heracles by way of worshipping his mythological father. The Ptolemies participated actively in the cult of Khonsu, identifying with the son of Amun by portraying themselves as divine children of the gods.

■ **Naos**

Red granite | Ptolemaic period
H. 110 cm | W. 53 cm | D. 63 cm

Discovered in the waters of Heracleion, this naos was likely a monument to Khonsu, a god associated with the moon.

Franck Goddio and his team lift the head of a Ptolemaic king onto their ship, excited to begin the work of restoration.

■ Statuette of Athena

Bronze | Ptolemaic period
H. 9.2 cm | W. 2.8 cm | D. 1.4 cm

Ancient Egyptians associated the Greek
goddess Athena with the Egyptian Neith,
their goddess of wisdom. Statuettes such
as this one of Athena prove the influence
of Greek mythology on Egyptian religion
and religious practices.

■ Horus falcon emblem

Bronze | 6th–2nd c. B.C.
H. 6.9 cm | W. 1.4 cm | L. 4.2 cm

Horus, one of Egypt's oldest gods, stands in the form
of a falcon wearing the crown of Upper and Lower
Egypt. This god is son of Isis and Osiris, who Isis bore
after bringing her husband back to life after he had
been brutally dismembered by Set.

▨ Head of the vulture-goddess Nekhbet

Bronze | 6th–2nd c. B.C.
H. 17 cm | W. 10 cm | Th. 3 cm

The largest bird of prey in Egypt, the falcon lives on
limestone cliffs and hovers above the desert and the
delta regions to search for food. Nekhbet, goddess of
Upper Egypt, was represented as a vulture from the
fourth dynasty on. As theology evolved, Nekhbet was
associated with the goddesses Mut, Hathor,
and Sekhmet.

▨ Anubis emblem

Bronze | 6th–2nd c. B.C.
H. 8.6 cm | L. 4.7 cm | Th. 2.7 cm

On this door emblem stands the canine Anubis,
the god of mummification and the journey into
the afterlife. Though difficult to discern because
his long pointed ears are broken, the lower part
consists of a cylinder that evokes a papyrus-style
column supporting the base of the emblem itself.

▨ Sacred bull emblem

Bronze | 6th–2nd c. B.C.
H. 4.5 cm | W. 1.6 cm | L. 4.2 cm

The sacred bull of Memphis, named Apis by the
Egyptians, was revered by all who beheld him. The
base of the horns and what seems to be a part of a
solar disk emerge slightly from this emblem. Many
figurines similar to this one have been discovered in
the Bay of Aboukir and surrounding areas.

A diver contemplates a statuette of Bastet underwater.

Holes caused by corrosion perforate the neck of this bronze statuette of the cat goddess Bastet. The lower part of the animal is lost, but the shape of the head and the ears clearly denote a sacred feline.

Statues and statuettes similar to this one were used as votive offerings to the goddess Bastet herself, who was a protectress of Upper and Lower Egypt, as well as a symbol of feminine fertility and pleasure. The worship of Bastet dated back to the Old Kingdom, around 2600 B.C. According to myth, Bastet was the daughter of the sun god, Re. The significance of the goddess evolved over time—some even said that Bastet was the representation of the soul of Cleopatra's chosen goddess, Isis—but she was almost always depicted with the head of a cat and the body of a woman. Cats were demigods to Egyptians, who outlawed the harming or killing of cats, making these offenses punishable by death. Bronze statues and statuettes of this goddess are distributed throughout dozens of museums and private collections: like Osiris and Isis lactans figures, they exist in the hundreds. Nevertheless, the high volume of these figurines indicates that the importance of the goddess Bastet was equivalent to that of Osiris and Isis.

■ **Statuette of the cat Bastet**

Bronze | 6th–2nd c. B.C.
H. 19 cm | W. 4.3 cm | D. 7.1 cm

The sacred cat Bastet sits perched, as if in acknowledgment of her worshippers.

Statuette of Khonsu with lunar disk

Bronze | Egyptian Late Period
H. 21.5 cm | W. 6.5 cm

The short loincloth, forward stride, and tripartite nemes headdress worn by this statuette are all principal characteristics of the god Khonsu. Khonsu was compared to the left eye of his father, Amun, and was seen as a heavenly body providing nocturnal light. A lunar disk sits above the nemes, illuminating his path.

Head of Osiris

Bronze | Egyptian Late Period
H. 5.5 cm | W. 1.5 cm | Th. 2 cm

God of the dead, the underworld, and resurrection, Osiris wears the white atef crown, flanked by two ostrich feathers, the symbol of Ma'at. Above the forehead rises the royal cobra.

Statuette of Bastet

Bronze | 6th–2nd c. B.C.
H. 7.1 cm | W. 3.9 cm | D. 1.6 cm

Here, we can see another example of a statuette representing Bastet as a woman with the head of a cat. The body of the goddess is cut off at the level of the pelvis, and judging from the circular hole in the right hand, the goddess used to hold an object, most likely a sistrum.

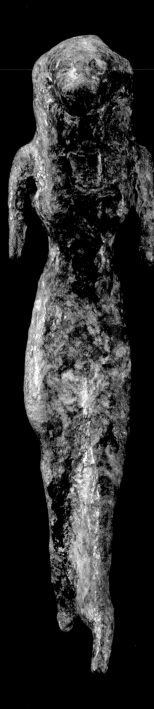

■ **Statuette of Sekhmet**

Bronze 6th–2nd c. B.C.
H. 16.7 cm | W. 3.7 cm | D. 1.7 cm

With the head of a lioness, Sekhmet unleashed
her anger to drive back the serpent Apophis and
destroy the enemies of Re, thus contributing
to maintaining cosmic balance. In the representations in Ptolemaic temples, the king, who
established himself as the son of the goddess,
went every day to the appeasement rites held
in her honor.

▪ Coin

Silver | 4th c. B.C.
Diam. 2.4 cm | Wt. 15.16 g

An owl stands to the right of the obverse of this coin; behind, an olive branch hangs, a statement of peace, despite the image of Athena on the head of the coin (not shown).

▪ Tetradrachm

Silver | Ptolemy I (310–306 B.C.)
Diam. 2.7 cm

The reverse side of this coin depicts Athena advancing in battle, holding a lance in the right hand and a shield in the left. In front of her is an eagle, guarding this Greek goddess from harm's way.

▪ Coin

Bronze | Ptolemaic period
Diam. 1.7 cm | Wt. 4.94 g

Also produced during the time of Ptolemy I Soter (304–283 B.C.), this coin was minted in the capital city of Alexandria. Alexander the Great is featured on the coin's head, in a tribute to the original liberator of Egypt from the Persians.

The reverse of this coin features Zeus's eagle, which became a symbol of the Ptolemaic dynasty.

■ Coin

Bronze | Ptolemaic period
Diam. 2.75 cm

Although this coin was produced in the mint of
Alexandria during the reign of Ptolemy I Soter,
the likeness on the head of the coin is not the
king but Zeus, king of the Greek gods. Egypt's first
Ptolemaic king, Ptolemy I Soter was regarded as
a savior because he maintained freedom from
Persian rule.

This phiale, or shallow dish, is the only gold vessel to have been recovered from underwater Heracleion, and it is remarkably complete and in good condition, with some minor dents in the sides and base. The vessel is simple, with a flat bottom and vertical sides. The central boss projects up a couple of millimeters from the base and has a flattened top surface. The vessel was made from one sheet of gold, most probably hammered into shape and then finished with a lathe.

Phialae were used throughout the Hellenistic world both for drinking and for pouring libations. Libation, the most frequent form of sacrifice in the ancient world, commonly involved two vessels: the wine jug and the phiale. Wine was poured from the jug into the dish, which was then tipped to allow the liquid to spill onto the ground.

The literary record confirms that phialae, especially in gold, were also used as diplomatic gifts. The vessel shape seems to have originated in post-Homeric times. There are ample references to the term in ancient literature and the word often occurs in the temple inventories, suggesting the shape was a favorite gift for the gods.

This phiale was found trapped beneath construction blocks of a traditional pharaonic-style temple and was likely used at this site as a part of the rituals taking place there or as a dedication.

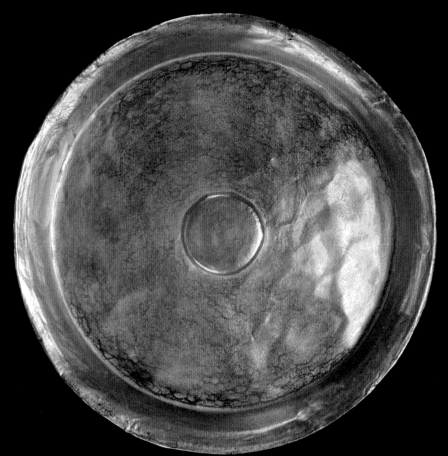

■ **Phiale**

Gold | 6th–2nd c. B.C.
H. 1.5 cm | Diam. 18.9 cm
Th. 0.1 cm | Wt. 172 g

The brilliant gold of this phiale was revealed by scientists who discovered it at Heracleion.

Tilting the phiale back and forth in the light, a diver's face is illuminated by his discovery.

■ Oil lamp

Lead | 5th–4th c. B.C.

This simple circular oil lamp is pinched
in one side in order to form a handle.
The same design is seen in ceramic oil
lamps of the period.

■ Box with miniature amphora and vessel

Lead | 6th–2nd c. B.C.
H. 3.5 cm | Diam. 5 cm

These miniature containers, like amulets,
were offered to the divinities. They served
as fragile and moving proof of fulfilled vows.

■ Vessel with oblation

Lead | 6th–2nd c. B.C.
H. 2.8 cm | Diam. 7 cm

This small receptacle held an offering to the deity. It was probably creased by the hands of the donor in order to keep the contents inside.

■ Platter

Lead | 6th–2nd c. B.C.
Diam. 14.5 cm

Although distorted and encrusted with debris from its centuries underwater, this platter was very likely a useful everyday object in someone's household.

■ Feeding bottle

Lead | 6th–2nd c. B.C.
H. 2.5 cm | Diam. 5 cm

Historians call vessels such as this one feeding bottles, presuming that the small, funneled opening was used to feed the young or the infirm.

Researchers lift a six-ton statue of Hapy, god of the Nile flood, out of the sea.

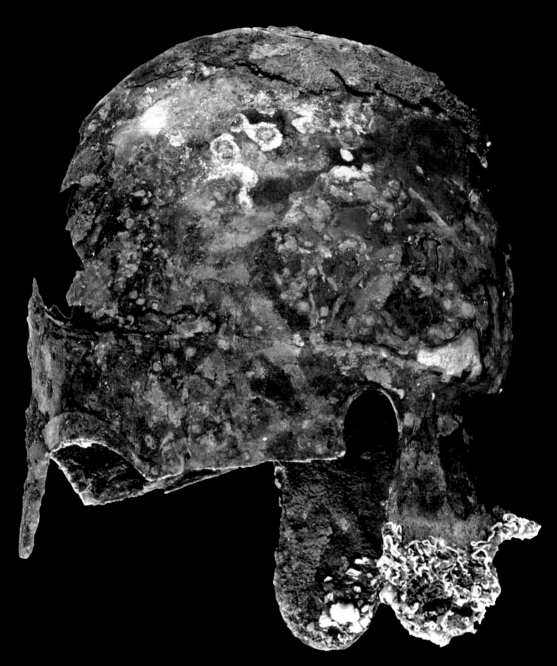

▪ Helmet

Bronze | 5th–4th c. B.C.
H. 34 cm | W. 23.5 cm

Helmets created in the Chalcidian style were
common during the late archaic period in
Greece (circa 650–500 B.C.). This helmet
resembles the well-known Corinthian helmet
in its curving ridge that separates the upper
and lower skull, and the decorative eyebrows
worked on the skull above either side of the
nasal guard.

■ Helmet crest

Bronze | 4th c. B.C.
H. 81 cm | W. 34 cm | D. 5 cm

Athena was depicted as wearing
a Corinthian-type helmet, a crest on top.
The style and workmanship of this example
suggest that it belonged to a large statue of
Athena from the fourth century B.C.

■ Helmet cheek piece

Bronze | 4th c. B.C.
H. 14 cm | W. 7.5 cm

Phrygian helmets took the shape of an elongated
lobe. They had hinged cheek pieces with two curves
cut out of the front edge, often decorated with false
beards and mustaches, as shown in the one above.

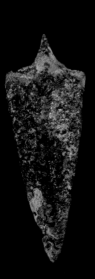

■ Arrowheads

Bronze | 6th–4th c. B.C.
L. 3 cm | Diam. 1.8 cm
L. 3.3 cm | W. 1.3 cm | D. 0.9 cm

Cretan archers were famous and served throughout the Mediterranean as mercenaries. The shape
of their arrowheads—with two deadly barbs on
either side—may have been adopted by other
Greek peoples and exported.

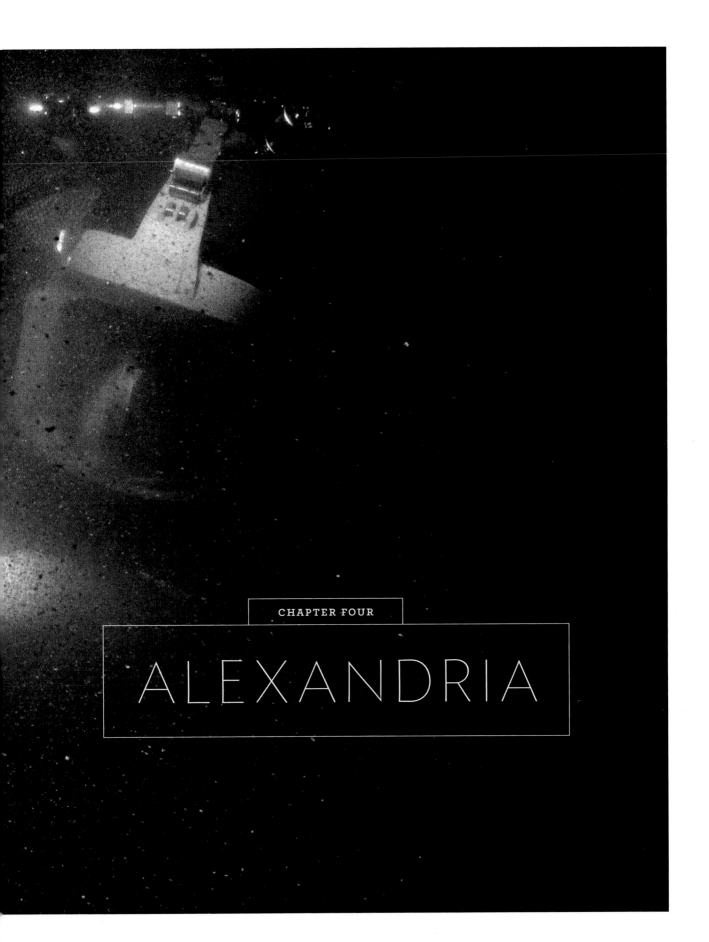

CHAPTER FOUR

ALEXANDRIA

THE ROYAL RESIDENCE of
CLEOPATRA

Franck Goddio

S oon after Cleopatra's death in 30 B.C., Greek historian and geographer Strabo came to live in Alexandria, Egypt's Portus Magnus—great port—and the dwelling place of the Ptolemaic rulers. From him we learn many details of how sumptuous the royal residences were. "The city holds splendid parks and the royal buildings," wrote Strabo, "for each of the kings, anxious to beautify in turn the public edifices with some new ornament, was no less eager to add, at his own cost, a new residence to those existing already." The royal city was a work in progress, changing as each Ptolemaic ruler added eternal evidence of his or her reign. Egypt's last queen, Cleopatra VII, epitomized this practice. Although the Portus Magnus now rests on the seafloor, the artifacts that researchers have uncovered, combined with the literary record of this famous queen, show Cleopatra's residence to be at the center of a bustling commercial hub and a point of cultural convergence for Romans, Greeks, and Egyptians.

The sumptuous complex of palaces and gardens—together known as the basileia, or royal palace—was located on Cape Lochias, which protected the Portus Magnus to the east. Adjacent to these palaces was the Royal Library, the temple of Poseidon, and the Caesarium, a building dedicated to the glory of Julius Caesar by order of Cleopatra herself. As a further testament to her power and extravagant tastes, Cleopatra also had a palace on the island of Antirhodos, inside the harbor. The island had its own small port for the exclusive use of the royal family.

In 1992, IEASM initiated research on the sunken port of Alexandria, determined to perform a comprehensive survey of this underwater site. Pollution and natural sedimentation forced researchers to develop new methodologies for interpreting the submerged landscape. By dating the foundations of buildings found in the port, scientists confirmed

Strabo's observation that the Portus Magnus was constantly being rebuilt throughout the Ptolemaic period. The structures of the port were planned around the well-defined contours of the coastline and the commercial activities that went on there. Docks, dikes, wharves, and jetties now lie underwater, representing the Portus Magnus of Cleopatra's day. A geological analysis of the sediments upon which the port was built has revealed that many collapsed buildings now lie approximately 8 meters below the ancient ground level and up to 6 meters below the present-day sea level. To envision the ancient port of Cleopatra's time, archaeologists also need to understand how it came to be submerged.

UNDERWATER ALEXANDRIA

State-of-the-art electron detection devices—magnetometers using nuclear magnetic resonance technology, for example—help portray the processes of change that the sites have undergone since Cleopatra's day. It is generally acknowledged that the sea level in Alexandria has risen by 1 to 1.5 meters over the past two millennia, and the land level has dropped 5 to 6 meters in that same period of time. But investigation suggests that some sort of short-term cataclysmic sediment failure occurred here as well. We know that that portion of the Mediterranean seafloor has been earthquake-prone, due to the subduction of the African plate under the Anatolian plate, and ancient texts describe specific earthquakes and tsunamis. The Roman historian Ammianus Marcellinus, for example, recorded details of a tsunami that rocked Alexandria in A.D. 365. "The whole earth was made to shake and shudder," he wrote. Huge ships were thrown a mile or two inland onto the roofs of houses in Alexandria. Other significant earthquakes were reported in the 8th and 14th centuries, the latter toppling the famous lighthouse that guided ships into Alexandria's harbor.

Despite good surveys and photographs, it was impossible to recognize the ruins of specific palaces and temples underwater in the Alexandria area. The region presented a sort of wasteland cluttered with collections—some dense, some sparse, some from dis-membered or partially demolished buildings—together with some stray sculptures and inscribed stones dating back to pharaohs prior to Alexander. But by comparing a detailed map of the archaeological remains to the literary record, researchers have identified build-ings and configurations such as the royal port, the island of Antirhodos, the ancient sea-walls, and the Timonium Palace where Cleopatra and Mark Antony courted one another.

While the seafloor leaves us with a somewhat incomplete portrait of Cleopatra's palace, the literary record tells us more about her exquisite living quarters. One can only dream of the description written by Roman poet Lucan, who describes huge slabs of marble, agate, and porphyry, with onyx floors and ebony doorjambs, "like a temple of luxury." Lucan's description is poetry and not history, but the materials he names are probably accurate, the stuff of splendor manifesting the cultural and commercial success of Alexandria.

Excavations in the eastern port have revealed extraordinary vestiges of statuary that help us understand the religious world of ancient Alexandria and the cultural connections between Egypt's pharaonic past and the Greco-Roman present of Cleopatra's reign. One statue, found almost intact, portrays a priest grasping a vessel that contains the relics of Osiris. Another, found in the zone of the basileia, is a royal colossal statue of Caesarion, the eldest son of Cleopatra and only son of Julius Caesar, together with two classical sphinxes. All were carved from either granite or diorite. Standing before royal or religious structures, the sphinxes were used to proclaim the sovereign's divine power. One bears the image of King Ptolemy XII, the father of Cleopatra. Pharaonic and Greco-Roman styles overlap in a blend characteristic of this period, reflecting the heightened cultural exchange between Egypt and the Mediterranean world that occurred under Cleopatra and her forebears.

The western section of the Portus Magnus contains a large port with several separate harbors, and these facilities contributed to the city's strength as an epicenter of political and commercial activity. The Ptolemaic navy was one of the most powerful in the Mediterranean. A secure base and extensive naval dockyards in the Portus Magnus helped to ensure the Ptolemies' continued supremacy on the high seas.

CENTER OF TRADE

Alexandria's Portus Magnus was also the greatest commercial hub of the eastern Mediterranean in the time of Cleopatra. To the east, Lake Mariotis linked the city to the Nile by a series of canals, enabling the movement of agricultural products from the fertile hinterlands to the city, ensuring both subsistence and prosperity. Merchandise from throughout Egypt, the Red Sea, India, and China traveled by canal into Alexandria. Thus the city linked Egypt with the Mediterranean Sea, the Indian Ocean, the Nile Valley, and Africa. Numerous imported ceramic objects brought up from the seafloor leave no doubt as to the plethora of wares from all directions traded in Alexandria.

International exchanges, with Alexandria at the crossroads, spurred the development of coins in Egypt. In 326–325 B.C., a workshop was set up in Alexandria, most likely near the basileia. A monetary policy was put into place in 323 B.C. by Ptolemy I, and continued by his successors, imposing strict oversight and the systematic conversion of foreign currency into Ptolemaic currency. Bronze coins of different denominations were generally used for daily trading. The bearded head of Zeus-Amun appears most often on them; on the reverse, the eagle with spread or folded wings. The legend reads "Ptolemaiou Basileios"—of King Ptolemy. The issue of bronze coins declined during the second century B.C. but picked up again during the reign of Cleopatra. The coins from her era, which weighed less than earlier Ptolemaic coins, appear relatively frequent in current collections and at archaeological sites.

These coins provide us with the rare opportunity to view the profile of this great queen—one of the few, if not the only, true portraits of the legendary last pharaoh of Egypt. Those who came after her did their best to destroy her visage and legacy, leaving very few images of Cleopatra existing today. Even the minuscule imprints on these bronze coins are only thought to portray her because they circulated during her reign. Thus this great queen remains shrouded in mystery, left up to the imaginations of artists, historians, and film directors.

It is telling that one of the only images of Cleopatra comes to us embedded in the currency of the time. From handsome jewels to ceramic vessels to steadfast sphinxes, her palace was filled with the treasures of her era. Her home was an oasis of luxury, and the Portus Magnus of Alexandria was the conduit through which these riches flowed. Perhaps only the beauty of Cleopatra herself could rival that of her living quarters. ∎

> "How I loved. . . .
> One day passed by, and nothing saw but love;
> Another came, and still 'twas only love:
> The suns were wearied out with looking on,
> And I untired with loving.
> I saw you every day, and all the day;
> And every day was still but as the first,
> So eager was I still to see you more."
>
> — MARK ANTONY IN JOHN DRYDEN, *All for Love* (1677)

PAGES *134-135*: A white marble head of Antonia Minor, Mark Antony's daughter, lies in Alexandria's waters.

■ **Coin**

Bronze | Cleopatra VII (51–30 B.C.)
Diam. 2.1 cm | Wt. 8.37 g

One of the only existing images of Cleopatra
produced during her life, this bronze coin depicts
the head of Cleopatra wearing a diadem, or crown.
The coin remains symbolic of Alexandria's
prosperity while she was queen.

■ Coin

Gold | Ptolemy I (305–283 B.C.)
Diam. 1 cm

The first of the Ptolemies adorns the head of
this gold coin, facing to the right with diadem
and aegis. The reverse shows an eagle on
a thunderbolt, its wings open, ready to fly
away. Researchers discovered several other
similar coins at their site in Alexandria
(following page).

These coins have the first of the
Ptolemies on one side, an eagle clasp-
ing a thunderbolt on the obverse.

■ **Stater from Cyrene**

Gold | Ptolemy I (304–283 B.C.)
Diam. 1.74 cm | Wt. 7.14 g

The head of Ptolemy I, with diadem and aegis around his neck, appears on one side of this coin.
The other side bears a Greek inscription as well as the glorified figure of Alexander the Great, who holds a bundle of lightning bolts in his right hand and stands on a chariot drawn by four elephants.

■ **Cypriot hemistater**

Gold | circa 354 B.C., reign of Pumiyaton
Diam. 1.37 cm | Wt. 4.10 g

On the face of this coin, a lion leaps onto the back of a stag and sinks its teeth into the base of the wild animal's neck. The obverse features Heracles walking, naked except for the lion skin covering his head and his arm as he draws back his bow and brandishes his club.

The priest stands on the ocean floor, among the structural ruins of Alexandria.

This beautiful sculpture carved from dark granitoid rock was found on the southwestern shore of the island of Antirhodos in the eastern port of Alexandria. The statue was touching a paved area and a mass of fallen rocks, a short distance from the two sphinxes of the Ptolemaic period. The figure is wearing a cloak tightly wrapped around the upper body, including the arms, over a long pleated tunic. The lower part is missing from the ankles down; a cylindrical mortise in the center of this fracture was surely the trace of an ancient attempt at restoration after a break that occurred in antiquity.

In his two hands, hidden under the folds of his cloak, the young man carries a vase pressed against his cheek at the height of his shoulders. This type of vase, made with a round body and a human head on top, is called an Osiris-Canopus jar. The sculpture thus represents a young priest bearing a divine image, most likely during a procession or a cultic ceremony.

This statue confirms the literary record that refers to the liturgical use of vases in ancient Egyptian processions. More importantly, this statue is part of an iconographic development, and it informs the theological backdrop for Cleopatra's rule. The tender way the priest carries the Osiris-Canopus vase, resting it lightly on his cheek, evokes a love for the god and a desire to forever remain in his presence.

Priest with Osiris-Canopus jar

Black granite | 1st c. B.C.
H. 122 cm

This priest holding an Osiris-Canopus jar was among the most important works of art discovered in the waters of Alexandria.

■ Mortar

Granodiorite | 6th–2nd c. B.C.
H. 30 cm | Diam. 32 cm

Mortars (right and below) and pestles
(below right) made of granite and volcanic
hard rock were used for food preparation.

■ Mortar

Granodiorite | 6th–2nd c. B.C.
H. 14 cm | Diam. 37.5 cm

These everyday items were likely to have been
found in open work areas such as the kitchen
or the courtyard.

■ Pestle

Granodiorite | 6th–2nd c. B.C.
H. 27 cm | Diam. 9.1 cm

The pestle, which ground seeds, herbs,
or other dry food materials into powder,
was made of hard stone and shaped to
fit inside an accompanying mortar.

Colossal head

Granodiorite | 1st c. B.C.
H. 80 cm | W. 60 cm | D. 50 cm

Statues that were Egyptian in style but adopted key Greek features began to surface during the reign of Ptolemy V, and continued to be made through the rule of Cleopatra. This head is likely a representation of Caesarion, Cleopatra's son by Julius Caesar. He wears a nemes, signifying his royalty, and bears certain features found on the coins and other representations of his mother.

■ **Sphinx**

Diorite | 1st c. B.C.
H. 75 cm | L. 140 cm

The traditional pose of the Egyptian sphinx has the front feet
stretched forward with the back legs tucked up underneath the
body. This example is no exception; the flanks are powerful and
the belly is drawn in. But it is the sphinx's head that catches one's
attention, because in many cases it represents the sovereign
ruling at the time the sphinx was produced. The head wears the
royal nemes, with traces of the royal uraeus still visible on the front.
Scientists believe the sphinx's origins to be local, perhaps even
around Alexandria.

■ Sphinx (Ptolemy XII)

Granodiorite | 1st c. b.c.
H. 70 cm | L. 150 cm

The face of this sphinx blends pharaonic traditions with Hellenistic portraiture style, a defining characteristic of statues produced in the later part of the Ptolemaic period. The unique treatment of the hair is characteristic of the numismatic portraits of Ptolemy XII Auletes Neos Dionysus. Thus the sphinx may in fact be a royal statue of Cleopatra's father, who squandered the money of the Egyptian people on bribes in order to keep the Romans content. Nevertheless, without the decree written by Ptolemy XII just before his death, Cleopatra might never have ascended to the throne.

Diver and sphinx come face to face in the sunken remains of Alexandria's eastern harbor.

Amulet in the form of an Osiris *hydreios*

Lead-filled bronze | Roman period
H. 6 cm | L. 2.2 cm | D. 1.9 cm

In Egypt the depiction of deities in the form of human-headed water jars probably began in the first century A.D. The idea that one would quench one's thirst by drinking from this jar emphasizes the rejuvenating effects of worshipping the deity Osiris.

A female deity, likely the goddess Ma'at, squats on a four-footed pedestal. A slight protuberance is visible at the top of her head, probably the beginning of an ostrich plume, the emblem of the deity.

Ma'at represents both truth and justice, but is also the goddess of social, societal, and political order. Originating in the Old Kingdom, this goddess added an ethical dimension to ancient Egyptian spirituality. The Egyptians believed that the universe had a defined order and organization; without Ma'at, chaos would ensue. Her principal role during the time of the pharaohs was to assure the permanence of the monarchy and the safety and stability of the world.

In return for the security that Ma'at assured each new pharaoh, the incoming ruler would always pledge devotion to Ma'at prior to taking the throne. It is also said that in Egyptian courts of law, the judge was labeled a "priest of Ma'at," and wore Ma'at's signature ostrich plume, awarding it to whomever won the case at the end.

Ma'at also played a role in the afterlife. According to myth, when a person died, the god Thoth weighed the heart of the deceased on a scale balanced on one side by Ma'at. If the scale showed that the person in question had been faithful to Ma'at, then he or she would go on to the afterlife. If, however, the scale did not balance, it revealed that the deceased had gone against Ma'at during life—and a demon would unflinchingly devour that person's heart.

■ **Figurine of the goddess Ma'at**

Bronze | 6th–2nd c. B.C.
H. 8.5 cm | W. 2.5 cm | D. 1.9 cm

Ma'at was one of the many female deities worshipped in ancient Egypt.

Unguentarium

Ceramic | 5th–4th c. B.C.
H. 9.5 cm | Diam. (opening) 2.5 cm | Th. 0.8 cm

An excellent example of Egyptian pottery, this unguentarium has a round base, and a roughly cylindrical body, neck, and plain rim. The pinkish clay has many fine nodules of oxidized iron.

Rhodian amphora

Ceramic | Roman period
H. 98.5 cm | Diam. 29.5 cm
Diam. (opening) 12 cm

The pointed base, tapered body, angled handles, and round cross section of this Rhodian amphora all suggest that this vessel belongs to the last production phase of Rhodian workshops in the first to second century A.D.

Bowl

Ceramic | 2nd c. B.C.
H. 6 cm | Diam. 13 cm | Th. 0.5 cm

This Ptolemaic Egyptian ceramic bowl shows the influence and adoption of foreign models, in this case from the Greek world

■ Oil lamp

Ceramic | Late 4th–early 3rd c. B.C.
H. 4.3 cm | Diam. 3.4 cm | Th. 1.7 cm

Like all the lamps with preserved spouts found throughout the Alexandrian excavation site, this one has soot smudges, leftover traces of its use. The lamp is an Alexandrian production inspired by Athenian lamps.

■ Amphora from the Circle of Clazomenae

Ceramic | Late 7th c.–6th c. B.C.
H. 42.5 cm | Diam. (opening) 10.5 cm | Th. 1.5 cm

Identified at Heracleion and dated between the late seventh century and the first three-quarters of the sixth century B.C., amphorae from the Circle of Clazomenae, north Ionia of Asia Minor, have been well preserved underwater.

■ Pot

Alabaster | 6th–2nd c. B.C.
H. 6.7 cm | Diam. 7.5 cm

Finer stones, such as alabaster, were used to make ointment and perfume containers.

Divers look down over the sphinxes and priest.

■ Epitaph in Greek of a soldier

Marble | Ptolemaic period
H. 20 cm | W. 20 cm | L. 45 cm

This inscribed white marble stone was found to the
west of the Grand Canal at Heracleion. The absence
of a notch in the stone suggests that it was not the
base of a statue, but a tombstone inserted in the
wall of a vault. The four Greek lines inscribed refer
to Homeric poetry, endowing this particular epitaph
with both literary and historical significance.

■ Headrests

Limestone | 6th-2nd c. B.C.
H. 17-19.5 cm | W. 10.1-11 cm | L. 26.5-27 cm

These limestone headrests are trapezoidal with a
concave surface. The shape is familiar in headrests
of a more modest size since the Old Kingdom.

Stone represented a natural material with a wide range of uses in ancient Egypt. The geographical positioning of the land allowed various natural veins of stone to be explored and mined as early as the predynastic period. Due to the landscape of Egypt, limestone is the most ubiquitous rock found and was the stone most often used for building construction and some statuary. Harder stones, which were more costly—such as granite and diorite—were often laboriously quarried in Aswan at the southern border of the country or in the Sinai.

These limestone headrests likely belonged to the more common citizens of Egypt from the Egyptian Late Period through the beginning of the Ptolemaic dynasty. The concave surface and general shape are familiar in headrests of a more modest size since the Old Kingdom. While royalty probably used more elegant instruments than this, Cleopatra likely used a headrest just like the rest of her kingdom.

The upper part, in the shape of a crescent, supported the head of the sleeper who would be lying on his side. This also allowed air to circulate around the head, providing relief from the warm Egyptian climate. Although the general shape could vary, many headrests had representations of guardian genies, who kept evil spirits away while the sleeper traveled into their dreams.

■ **Grindstone**

Volcanic rock | 6th-2nd c. B.C.
H. 10 cm | W. 42 cm | L. 65 cm

This grindstone was a practical tool likely used during the beginnings of the Ptolemaic period.

■ Head-shaped gold pendant

Gold | 3rd–2nd c. B.C.
H. 1.12 cm | W. 0.91 cm | D. 0.51 cm

The identity of the chubby face with almond-shaped eyes and rolled eyebrows on this piece of jewelry is unknown. Two parallel, horizontal grooves, the so-called Venus rings, are to be found on the throat. On the back, a piece of gold sheet covers the pendant.

■ Pendant in the shape of a *tabula ansata*

Gold | Late Roman or Byzantine period
L. 0.66 cm | W. 1.34 cm | D. 0.04 cm

This piece of gold sheet is shaped like a tabula ansata, or tablet with handles. Though similar to votive tablets from the Roman period, this tabula ansata has two eyelets on the back, suggesting that it was used as a pendant later in the Byzantine period.

■ Wedding ring

Gold | Byzantine period, 6th–8th c. A.D.
Ring: D. 2.2 cm | Th. 0.1 cm
Setting: D. 1.4 cm

The inscriptions on this gold ring read, "Peace, which is mine, I give to you. Amen." This is a quotation from the Gospel according to John (14:27). The setting depicts Christ with a halo, raising his right arm toward the shoulder of a young man and his left toward the shoulder of a young woman in order to initiate their union as husband and wife.

Bead in the shape of an Eye of Horus

Gold | Ptolemaic period
H. 0.68 cm | W. 0.18 | L. 0.82 cm

This bead consists of two pieces of gold sheet shaped as
an Eye of Horus. Necklaces with this image were popular
from the pharaonic period up through the Roman period.
Perhaps Cleopatra herself even wore this symbol, which
signified health and well-being to the Egyptian people.

Flanked by sphinxes on either side, the priest stands as if about to process through the murky water.

Ring

Gold and agate | Roman period
Diam. 2.29 cm

Consisting of a circular hoop made of gold sheet, this
ring has an oval setting containing a white-red agate
cabochon. Rings such as this one were popular at the
beginning of the Roman Imperial period, as examples
from Pompei may demonstrate.

Ring with oval glass or stone cabochon

Gold, glass, or stone | Ptolemaic period
Ring: Diam. 2.68 cm | Th. 1.89 cm
Cabochon: H. 1.45 cm | W. 0.96 cm | Th. 0.35 cm

A dark red—almost black—oval glass or stone cabochon
was found not far from this gold ring, the dimensions of
which correspond precisely to those of the setting. Rings
of this style were widespread throughout the Hellenic
world and up into the Roman period.

Ring

Gold | 1st c. B.C.–1st c. A.D.
Diam. 2.53 cm

The shipwreck in which this ring was found
contained pottery from the end of the first century
B.C. to the first century A.D. The polygonal ring with
a tiered bezel is undecorated except for some
engraved lines on the edges.

Ring with an engraved Victory

Gold | circa late 4th–early 3rd c. B.C.
Diam. 2.97 cm | Th. 2.8 cm

The goddess engraved in this gold ring appears to be Nike, the personification of victory. She stands close to an incense holder, presenting an offering of smoke. Nike shows that female deities, like female sovereigns in ancient Egypt, took on battles and often emerged victorious.

Ring made of one twisted wire

Gold
Diam. 1.56 cm | Th. 0.4 cm

A single twisted wire ends in a so-called Hercules knot, forming a unique gold ring. A similarly made bracelet was found together with other pieces of gold jewelry in Khusfin in southern Syria, one of the territories Cleopatra received from Mark Antony in return for financing one of his foreign campaigns.

Ring

Gold and semiprecious stone | 1st c. B.C.–1st c. A.D.
Ring: Diam. 2.95 cm
Setting: Diam. 1.8 cm

A hoop made of three massive beaded wires forms a spectacular golden ring fit for a queen. The oval bezel soldered to the ring contains a double-layered, dark blue and white intaglio. The engraved image shows a bird with a ribbon in its beak.

Researchers found an oval jar of white marble in the vicinity of two sphinxes. The jar had severely worn walls decorated in relief, and the top had been broken off. Not far away, the divers discovered the missing top in the form of a male head wearing a striated wig. The intricate jar was unmistakably an Osiris-Canopus jar, a sacred water jar used by priests in the cult of Isis during the Ptolemaic dynasty.

A religious scene decorates the belly of this jar. On two sides of the naos we can distinguish two pairs of naked figures of childlike proportions; one of these is likely Harpocrates, but it is difficult to identify the others. As one of Egypt's first fertility gods, Osiris blessed the water of the Nile with its rich nutrients that would make any plant grow. Although an instrument of the cult of Isis rather than her husband Osiris, these jars symbolized the growth and rebirth governed by Isis. This jar is from the Roman period, but it is not unlikely that similar vessels were carried by priests in Canopic processions when Cleopatra lived there with Mark Antony in order to shield their affair from the scrutiny of the public eye.

■ Osiris-Canopus jar

Marble | 1st–2nd c. A.D.
Vase: H. 24 cm | Diam. (upper) 21.2cm
Diam. (lower) 13 cm | Head: H. 13.3 cm
W. 12.6 cm | D. 11.1 cm

Sacred Osiris-Canopus jars such as this one, right, were used by priests and priestesses of the cult of Isis in their rituals and ceremonies.

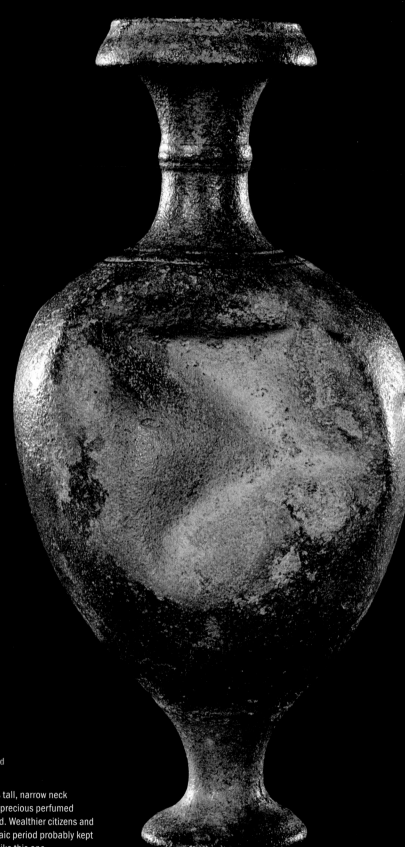

■ Vessel

Bronze | Ptolemaic period
H. 10.3 cm | D. 5.1 cm

This delicate receptacle's tall, narrow neck
prevented spillage of the precious perfumed
oils that it likely contained. Wealthier citizens and
royalty during the Ptolemaic period probably kept
expensive oils in vessels like this one.

■ Cauldron

Bronze | Ptolemaic period
H. 18 cm | D. 27.9 cm | L. 45.4 cm

With a straight neck and concave spout but no base or foot, this cylindrical pot likely rested on a tripod or support that held it above a fire. This shape is called a kakkabe in ceramics, as its angled horizontal handles extending away from the body differentiate it from other shapes.

■ Bowls

Bronze | 5th-2nd c. B.C.
H. 6.5-9.8 cm | D. 12.7-15.5 cm | Th. 0.2-0.4 cm

The accentuated ridge on these Ptolemaic bowls marks a break between their convex belly and their straight or slightly concave upper part. A decoration of petals or ovolos often circles the base of these types of bowls, which were widespread for hundreds of years prior to Cleopatra's day.

■ Mug

Ceramic | Ptolemaic period
H. 8.7 cm | D. 5.1 cm | Th. 0.4 cm

An uncommon Hellenistic form, only a few mugs such as this have been found in the north of Egypt. These mugs date to the Ptolemaic period.

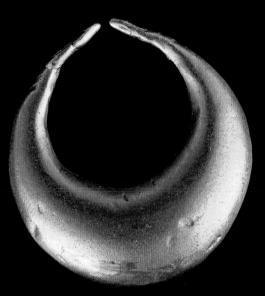

■ Sickle-shaped earring

Gold and filling material | Ptolemaic period
D. 2.65 cm | Th. 0.83 cm

Composed of two gold sheets and a filling material,
this earring is of the style that Cleopatra may have
worn as a Ptolemaic queen.

■ Earring with a granule pyramid

Gold | Ptolemaic period
D. 1.71 cm | Th. 0.55 cm

The granule pyramid that has been fastened to
this gold ring contains 18 equally sized granules.
The earring is an open hoop, and its ends overlap
to hold it in place.

■ Animal-headed earring

Gold | 3rd c. B.C.
D. 1.9 cm | Th. 0.38 cm

A tapered hoop fashioned from a gold sheet curves
out from the striking animal head mounted at the
top of this unique earring. The animal's eyes and
mouth are simple punchings in the gold, while the
ears and horns are also made of gold sheet.

Linked necklace

Gold | Late 6th–early 8th c. A.D.
L. 0.06–5 cm | W. 0.57–1 cm | Th. 0.13–0.25 cm

The largest circular link of one of three fragments found of this necklace bears a Greek cross, indicating that this stunning piece of jewelry comes from the Byzantine period. The pieces of this necklace and two similar bracelets are rumored to have been found in Egypt.

Cross pendant

Gold | 6th–early 8th c. A.D.
H. 1.51 cm | W. 0.94 cm | Th. 0.1 cm

This Latin cross has drop-shaped arms and an open eye made of a strip of wire. The arms of the cross are adorned with circular, drop-shaped and sickle-shaped punchings. Similar pieces hang on a lace-like necklace from the same time period.

Earring

Gold | Late Roman or Byzantine period
D. 1.3 cm | Th. 0.18 cm

A simple hoop earring, this piece has a circular cross section that decreases toward both ends. Such earrings were used over a long time period in ancient Egypt and were a relatively common fashion.

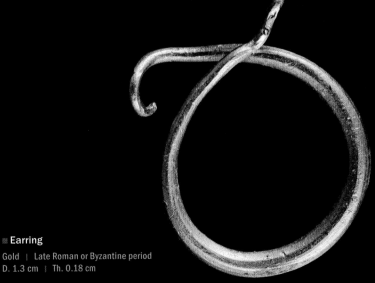

CHAPTER FIVE

CLEOPATRA

QUEEN of BEAUTY &
POWER

Zahi Hawass

When Cleopatra took the throne after the death of her father, Egypt was severely weakened, significantly in debt, and experiencing high inflation. The Nile had recently flooded more destructively than usual. Political power lay in the hands of Rome, and the feelings of Alexandrians toward the pharaoh had built to a fever pitch of anger and rebellion. Cleopatra rose to the occasion, entering the political arena with a strong character, a sharp mind, and feminine charms that she did not hesitate to use.

Cleopatra's mother remains a mystery, but we do know that she came from a long line of fearless Ptolemaic females who often participated in public affairs. At that time, strong leadership required a thorough education, including mathematics, writing, and full schooling on the laws and customs of Egypt, Greece, and Rome. Cleopatra probably had several private tutors who prepared her to rule Egypt, but she also pursued academic interests of her own—science, philosophy, and women's issues.

Unlike her forebears, Cleopatra learned the native language of Egypt as well as Greek and the languages of other countries. "She could readily turn to whichever language she pleased," wrote Plutarch, "so that there were few foreigners she had to deal with through an interpreter, and to most she herself gave her replies without an intermediary."

Of Macedonian descent—as were Alexander the Great and all the Ptolemies and Cleopatras who preceded her—she chose to become Egyptianized in her dress and appearance. She linked herself with Isis, assuming the goddess's symbols as her own. She confirmed strong ties with Rome and established loyalty among Egyptians. Her reign marks one of the most important periods in the entire Ptolemaic dynasty.

CLEOPATRA & JULIUS CAESAR

When Julius Caesar traveled to Egypt in 48 B.C., Cleopatra's brother, Ptolemy XIII, had been plotting to seize control from his sister. Sensing the danger, she had fled to Palestine. Like his father before him, Ptolemy XIII stopped at nothing to please the Romans in power, and he arranged for the murder of Caesar's rival, Pompey. The rash act infuriated Caesar. Meanwhile Cleopatra, according to Plutarch, secretly returned to Alexandria, wrapped up in a Persian carpet. A soldier presented the carpet to Caesar, unrolling the beautiful Cleopatra, who impressed the great Roman leader with her bravery and beauty.

The next day, Caesar sent for young Ptolemy in order to decide which one, brother or sister, should hold the throne. When Ptolemy saw his sister side by side with the Roman ruler, he threw his crown on the ground and ran into the street, calling her a traitor.

Months of struggle ensued, with Ptolemy XIII and a younger sister, Arsinoe IV, pitted against Cleopatra and Caesar for control of Egypt. As Cleopatra and Caesar remained barricaded in the basileia, one of Arsinoe IV's advisors poured seawater into the cisterns, making the water undrinkable. Roman forces arrived, facing off against 50 Egyptian ships that attempted to control the port of Alexandria. Ultimately the Roman forces won, burning all the Egyptian vessels in a conflagration so immense that it reached the Royal Library and destroyed many precious volumes.

Amid the sea battle, Ptolemy XIII drowned. Caesar captured Arsinoe IV and sent her to Rome. He proclaimed Cleopatra the queen of Egypt and ordered her to marry Ptolemy XIV, her brother, not yet 12 years old, and reign with him as coregent. Caesar wintered in Egypt with Cleopatra, cruising the Nile and granting the island of Cyprus to her as a sign of commitment and alliance. On June 23, 47 B.C., Cleopatra gave birth to Caesar's son, whom she named Ptolemy XV Caesar, but whom the Egyptians called Caesarion, "Little Caesar." The three Ptolemies—Cleopatra, Ptolemy XIV, and Caesarion—lived in Caesar's palace in Rome for more than a year. When Roman senators assassinated Caesar, on March 15, 44 B.C., they secretly returned to Egypt.

CLEOPATRA & MARK ANTONY

In Rome in 43 B.C., Brutus and Cassius, who had plotted against Julius Caesar, were defeated by Octavius and Mark Antony, who agreed to divide the empire between them. Antony acquired the eastern part of the empire, including Egypt. He arranged a meeting with Cleopatra, at which she is said to have arrived dressed as the goddess Isis. She quickly won him over.

In the name of his love for Cleopatra, Antony killed the queen's sister Arsinoe IV and possibly also Ptolemy XIV, because as long as they were alive they were a threat to their sister's rule. Foreign relations soon took Antony away from his life with Cleopatra in Alexandria, and when he returned, he had married Octavia, sister of Octavius, to secure political power.

> *"She shall be buried by her Antony:*
> *No grave upon the earth shall clip in it*
> *A pair so famous."*
>
> — OCTAVIUS CAESAR, in William Shakespeare,
> *Antony and Cleopatra* (circa 1605)

In 37 B.C., Mark Antony appealed to Cleopatra to support his campaign in Syria. Leveraging her lover's desperation for a victory, she received Syria, Phoenicia, and Cyprus in exchange for the funds he needed. Antony's offensive ultimately failed, but Cleopatra's rule now stretched farther than ever before.

In Rome, tensions were mounting. Octavius advanced into Persia, part of Antony's eastern empire. Octavius accused Antony of giving Roman property and power to a foreign woman. Most Egyptians honored Antony, but they wanted Cleopatra to live in Alexandria rather than Rome. Octavius clearly considered his rival to be not only Mark Antony but also Cleopatra. After winning a battle against Octavius's forces in Armenia in 34 B.C., Antony returned to Alexandria for a victory celebration where he sat on a throne of gold next to Cleopatra on a throne of silver.

The Egyptian people allied with Antony against Octavius and encouraged him to return to Rome. Cleopatra traveled with his army, even though the Egyptians wanted her to stay in Egypt. She persuaded Antony to divorce Octavia, which caused a scandal among the Romans and incited Octavius to declare war. Antony's allies told him he must send Cleopatra back to Egypt. Octavius cast the war in terms of a revolt against Antony and his lover, Cleopatra. Visiting the temple of Mars, the war god, Octavius recited the traditional Roman declaration of war. Thus began the Battle of Actium, the ancient world's last great sea battle.

The famous battle took place on September 2, 31 B.C. Octavius brought war against Antony, whom he saw as the traitor who had raised his hand against his country for a woman. Octavius had 80,000 ground troops, 12,000 horsemen, and 250 warships. Antony faced him with at least 500 ships, 100,000 infantry, and 12,000 cavalry. The Roman leader Agrippa cut off all of Antony's supplies from Egypt and Syria. As disease began to spread among his troops, Antony was forced into a defensive strategy. Octavius—with smaller, more maneuverable ships—excelled in the sea battle. Antony's Roman allies began to abandon him soon after the battle began. Cleopatra's ships were in the rear, and when she could no longer bear to watch Antony's defeat, she retreated to Alexandria. Antony fled to

Egypt but his troops, feeling abandoned, fled to Macedonia. Antony had lost his political stature, and this defeat left Cleopatra to contemplate the future of her empire.

In Alexandria, she led everyone to believe that she had been victorious in battle; she arranged festivals and did what she could to organize her people against Octavius, while at the same time she hid her treasures, fearing invasion and worse. Scholars believe that Cleopatra offered Octavius the head of Antony in order to confirm a new alliance between Egypt and Rome. He answered by telling her to give Egypt over, and afterward he would decide her fate. The last message Cleopatra received from Octavius stated that he would leave her the throne and not kill her. She could not melt Octavius's heart as she had the hearts of two others. Antony defeated Octavius's forces in Aboukir in July of 30 B.C., but it was his last victory, for his soldiers continued to desert him. He invited Octavius to fight, but Octavius refused. All Antony could do was sit in the palace and wait for Octavius.

THE DEATH OF CLEOPATRA

Legend has it that Cleopatra gathered her treasures, entered her tomb with assistants and slaves, and sent a message to Antony that she had killed herself. Antony, distraught, tried to kill himself as well. He did not succeed, and when the news came that Cleopatra was not dead, he went to die in her arms.

Alexandria was in trouble after the death of Antony, and Octavius continued to try to find a way to force Cleopatra to surrender. He sent men to negotiate with her. He feared she might attempt suicide, and he wanted to take her back to Rome, to show his victory over her and Egypt. But Cleopatra decided to take control of her own fate. On August 12, 30 B.C., Cleopatra's servants were ordered to enter her room, one carrying a serpent in a basket. She left behind a letter to Octavius, expressing her wish that she be buried with her beloved Mark Antony. She chose a royal death, inflicted through the bite of a cobra, a sacred servant of the sun god and the protector of all kings. So Cleopatra followed Antony in death and maintained her sovereign dignity.

Some scholars believe that Octavius killed Cleopatra and that the stories of her suicide are mistaken. But the ferocious strength that this queen displayed throughout her life suggests that she would proceed as courageously to her death, taking her own life to preserve the legacy of her homeland. ■

PAGES *172-173:* The head of the colossus Hapy waits on the seafloor before being lifted to the surface.

As fish flit underwater, a diver pauses, awed by the majesty of the statue before him.

A certain sense of calm dignity surrounds this magnificent sculpture of an unidentified Ptolemaic queen. Slightly larger than life size, this headless woman wears thinly draped garments that gather at her shoulder in an Isis knot.

Upon its discovery, the identity of the statue was immediately proclaimed to be Isis of Menouthis, after whom this knot was named. But as time passed, it became clear that many Ptolemaic women associated themselves with the goddess Isis and had commissioned statues that transposed characteristics of the goddess onto their own likenesses. Isis was the sister and wife of the god Osiris and the mother of Horus, just as the Ptolemaic queens were wives of the kings and bore the heirs to the throne.

Though this statue was produced before Cleopatra, she was no exception to this rule. In fact, Cleopatra took the Isis comparison further than any of the Ptolemaic women before her. When she came to power, she declared herself the reincarnation of Isis and had many statues made depicting her as such. When Mark Antony came to visit her for the first time, Cleopatra dressed as Isis in order to win his affection. The queen depicted in this statue helped set the precedent for using images of Isis, and Cleopatra drew on this when she came into power.

■ **Statue of a queen**

Granodiorite | 3rd c. B.C.
H. 150 cm | W. 55 cm | D. 28 cm

The majestic dark queen wears an Isis knot on her flowing robes.

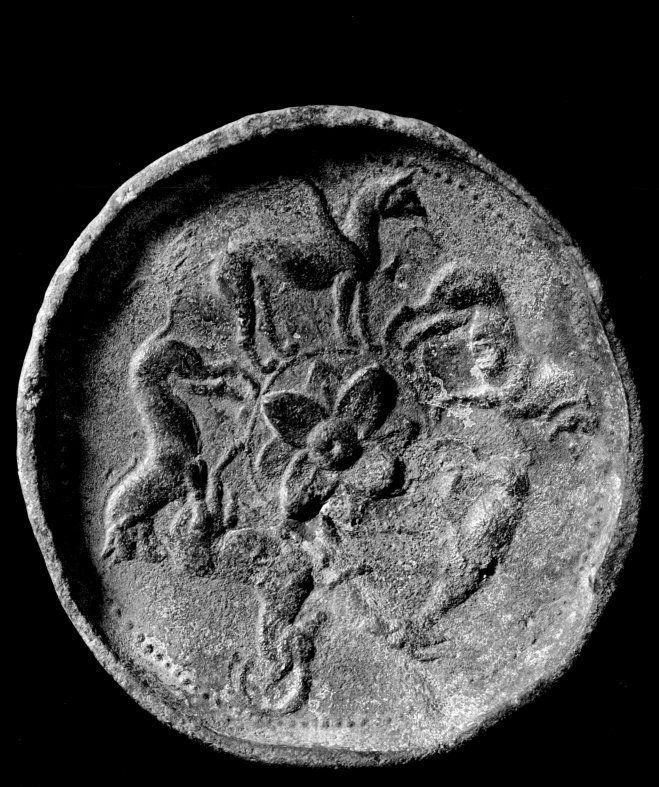

■ **Bowl**

Lead | Egyptian Persian period
H. 5 cm | Diam. 15 cm

The style of art produced in Egypt under Persian rule before Alexander the Great involved intricate decorations such as those lining the bottom of this flat lead bowl.

■ Coin

Bronze | Cleopatra VII (51–30 B.C.)
Diam. 2.5 cm

The profile of Cleopatra herself graces the head of this bronze coin produced sometime during her reign. Cleopatra's features are difficult to discern, only increasing the mystery behind this queen.
Reverse: An eagle stands on a thunderbolt.

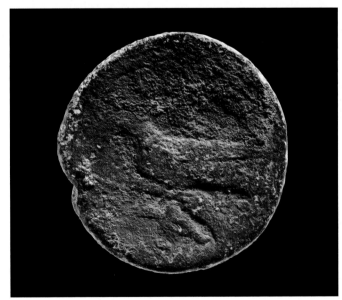

■ Earring with setting and two glass beads

Gold and glass | 5th–early 8th c. A.D.
L. 2.8 cm | W. 1.06 cm | Th. 0.07 cm

Two dark glass beads attached to a bent wire and a small bead made of a strip of gold sheet make a simple but elegant earring. The remains of a white substance that may have held the inlays together can be seen inside.

■ Pendant of an earring

Gold and pearls | 6th–early 8th c. A.D.
L. 8.7 cm | W. 0.95 cm | Th. 0.7 cm

Two pearls and in between a filigree bead are strung onto this wire pendant. This type of earring was popular in the Byzantine era.

■ Necklace with drop-shaped glass beads

Gold and glass | 6th–early 8th c. A.D.
L. 3.3 cm | W. 0.8 cm | Th. 0.8 cm

A drop-shaped violet glass bead attaches to each link, part of a larger necklace of repetitive design. Over a dozen such necklaces have been found in hoards buried in different parts of the Byzantine Empire.

■ Earring with two pendants

Gold and pearls | 6th–early 8th c. A.D.
L. 1.87 cm | W. 1.46 cm | Th. 0.31 cm

A broken pendant found with this gold hoop earring suggests that there was an additional pendant attached.

■ Pendant of an earring

Gold and pearls | 6th–early 8th c. A.D.
L. 5.25 cm | W. 0.5 cm | Th. 0.5 cm

Braided gold wire serves as the foundation of this pendant. A wire with a small bead of gold sheet and a larger pearl forms the second, more decorative part.

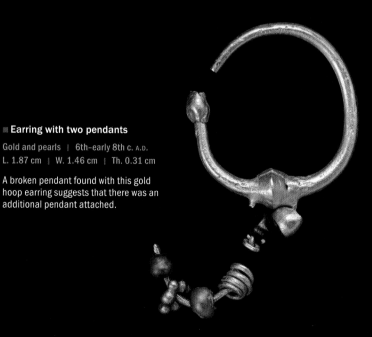

Rarely is an entire piece of ancient jewelry discovered, but fragments still tell a lot. All the pendants below consist of a single wire, to which different elements have been attached: a drop-shaped amethyst, pearls, and gold beads of different shapes. The rectangular setting (far right), made of gold sheet, wraps a green stone inlay, possibly an emerald. There are no traces of soldering anywhere, suggesting that these elements were created independently from any other piece of jewelry to which they might have been attached. Such pendants are found as part of earrings and necklaces dating from throughout the Roman and Byzantine periods.

Once the Romans took control of Egypt, jewelry styles began to change, and some of these pendants may postdate Cleopatra. The gold bead (third from left) resembles beads on earrings with S-shaped hooks found in a second-century A.D. grave in Tortosa, Syria. Pieces similar to the one with a purple bead (far left) appear to have been popular in the sixth and seventh centuries. Some hang, for instance, from a votive crown of the Visigoth king Reccesvinth, who ruled from A.D. 653 to 672.

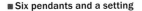 **Six pendants and a setting**

Gold, amethyst, green stone, pearls | Roman period–Byzantine period
L. 0.50-2.28 cm | W. 0.25-0.68 cm
Th. 0.24-0.47 cm

Six pendants reflect the variety of jewelry that existed in Egypt over centuries.

Hapy, god of the flood of the Nile, looms above underwater divers.

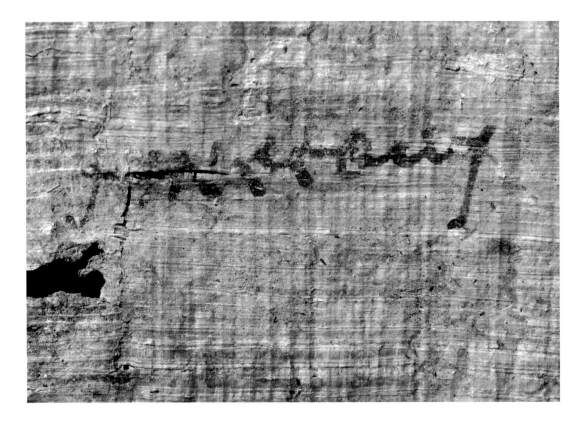

■ **Detail from ancient document**

First discovered at a gravesite near Cairo in 1904, this 2,000-year-old papyrus outlines a royal ordinance from the administration of Cleopatra. Its terms allowed wheat to be shipped duty-free out of Egypt in exchange for a substantial import of wine. Publius Canidius, who was an aide to Mark Antony, was the primary beneficiary of this agreement. Scientists believe that the scribble on the lower right of the document, shown in the detail above, was written by Cleopatra herself.

■ **Ancient document**

Papyrus | Ptolemaic period
L. 23.3 cm | W. 20.2 cm

Portions of this brief but concise note are thought to have been
written in Cleopatra's own hand. The Greek word *genethoi*,
which translates roughly to "let it be so," or "make it happen,"
appears below the written decree. As a ruler, Cleopatra knew
the inner workings of every part of her administration, making
it easy to interject an order to ensure a financial reward for her
lover's friend.

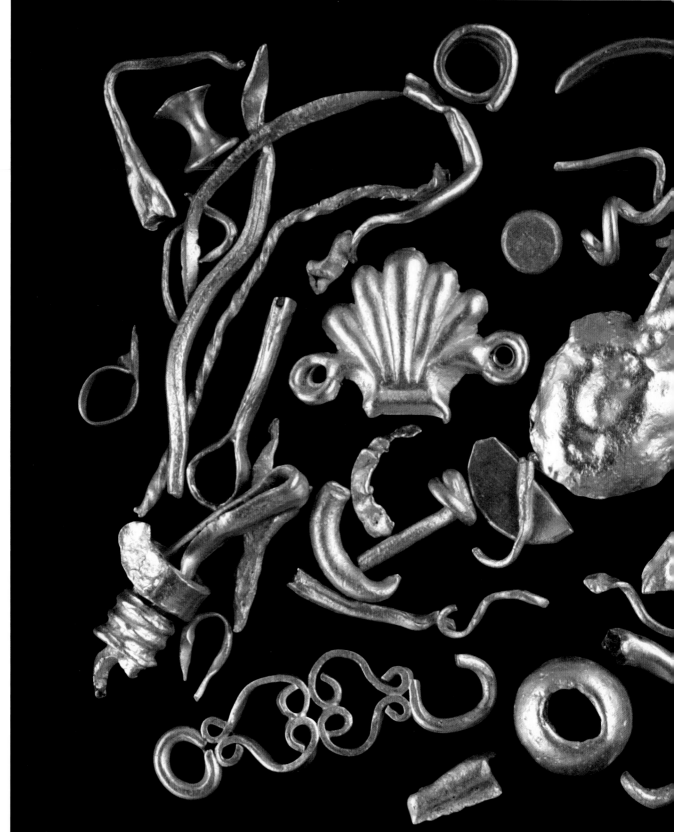

One can only imagine the splendor of Cleopatra's jewelry collection, which may have included gold pieces similar to these.

▨ Statuette of Harpocrates

Lead | Ptolemaic period
H. 4 cm | W. 2.5 cm

Harpocrates, son of Isis and Osiris, appears here as a nude, plump child, his left leg bent to the ground and the finger of his right hand lifted to his mouth. Under his left arm, the "divine child" holds a vessel containing the fruits of the earth that evoke his influence over the fertility of the land, like his parents.

▨ Statuette of Harpocrates

Lead | Ptolemaic period
H. 5 cm | W. 2.5 cm | D. 0.5 cm

The "divine child" Harpocrates was merely the Hellenized version of Horus. Thus, many statuettes depicting Harpocrates have a Hellenistic style. During the Ptolemaic dynasty, Horus and Harpocrates coexisted, just as the Egyptians and Greeks lived together.

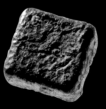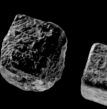

▨ Weights

Bronze | 6th–2nd c. B.C.
L. 0.3–1.2 cm | W. 0.3–1.2 cm | Wt. 0.45–7.13 g

These weights represent different weight standards. Heracleion was a harbor town, where trade activities involving different standards of measurement occurred on a daily basis.

Two shrines of Amun-Re and Khonsu-Heracles were discovered in the holy temple of Heracleion. Divers unearthed this red granite vat at the site. Two holes pierce its sides, one due to utilitarian reuse after the pagan period, and the other probably due to its use as a garden tank many years after that. Inside the vat, an image of Osiris was made from earth and mixed barley grains, which had been germinated and then exposed to the sun and dried. After it was made, its producers shipped the vat on a golden boat that brought it to the god's temple, which must have been located somewhere in the necropolis of Canopus. Then this obsolete "corpse" was disposed of, either buried with his predecessors in a collective hypogeum or thrown into the water.

Archaeologists are still researching the complexities of the rites carried out at Heracleion, yet it is clear that the now sunken city was the center of religion leading up to the time of Cleopatra. With its strong Greek influence, the hybridization of Egyptian and Greek deities—such as Amun-Re, Khonsu-Heracles, and Horus-Harpocrates—was reflected in religious ceremonies of Heracleion. Even the great god Osiris had his Greek and Roman counterparts in Dionysus and Baccus. This vat was merely a carrying case for a spiritual object, but it has now become a symbol of religious activity at Heracleion during the Ptolemaic era.

■ Vat

Red granite | Ptolemaic period
H. 63 cm | W. 90 cm | L. 205 cm

This vat originated as a spiritual item and was later repurposed for more practical uses.

Three divers line up beside this stone vat and behold the remains of Osiris.

As researchers fold back the layers of history in search of remnants of Cleopatra's age, they encounter artifacts from centuries before and after Cleopatra walked the Portus Magnus of Alexandria or worshipped in the temple of Heracleion. The pieces of pottery shown here were found in Heracleion and serve as examples of wares that preexisted the Ptolemaic queen by nearly three centuries. Some of these decorative vessels come from the very first settlers ever to come to the city to live; historical evidence shows that Heracleion was occupied continuously from the 26th dynasty up until the Ptolemaic period. The Ionian cup—and perhaps the table amphora—were likely brought over early in the 26th dynasty.

In general, the ceramics from Cleopatra's time range from the finest quality to undecorated and utilitarian. Ceramics were either imported or made locally in Egypt, often in Alexandria. Egyptian ceramics became more widespread under the Ptolemies, though the Greek amphorae maintained their importance as well. Nevertheless, Egyptian pottery took cues from the Greeks, imitating their shapes and production methods. While pottery made in Egypt before Alexander the Great did not incorporate Greek styles, the ceramic pieces on this spread prove the existence of Greek pottery in Egypt many years before.

■ **Red-figured vase**

Ceramic | 4th c. B.C.
H. 12 cm | Th. 0.7 cm

The bust of a man wearing a chlamys, or cloak, decorates this fragment of red pottery.

Kotyle

Ceramic | Late 5th–early 4th c. B.C.
H. 10 cm | Diam. 14.4 cm | Th. 0.7 cm

Two horizontal handles attach just under the rim of this ancient vessel. The rather wide ring base, diagonal walls, and straight rim define the structure of the kotyle. This ceramic was imported, perhaps from Asia Minor, where similar decorations have been discovered.

Ionian Cup

Ceramic | 6th c. B.C.
H. 6.3 cm | Diam. 15.7 cm | Th. 0.4 cm

Found at Heracleion, this fine Ionian drinking vase hails from a long eastern Greek tradition and was part of the first Greek settlements at Heracleion.

Painted table amphora

Ceramic | 5th c. B.C.
H. 32 cm | Diam. 22.5 cm |
Diam. (opening) 8.5 cm | Th. 0.6 cm

Geometrical decoration in brown to carmine red paint adorns the ring base and globular body of this table amphora. Rarely identified, the amphora is quite frequent among the fine ceramics of Heracleion from the pre-Ptolemaic period.

Crescent-shaped earring

Gold | 6th–early 8th c. A.D.
L. 2.65 cm | W. 2.18 cm | Th. 0.17 cm

The pierced work on the piece of gold sheet that comprises this crescent-shaped earring shows a drinking vessel from which vines are emerging. Discovered in the waters of Canopus, the gold is framed by beaded wire and attached to a hoop with a hook-and-eye closure.

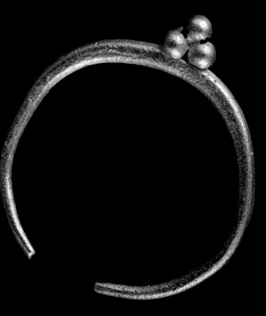

Earring with a pyramid of granules

Gold | 7th–early 8th c. A.D.
Diam. 1.4 cm | Th. 0.11 cm

The diameter of the open hoop that forms this earring tapers off at the ends. A pyramid of four granules rises from the hoop's base. Earrings with pyramids of granules were produced over a lengthy period of time in Egypt and throughout the Roman Empire. Cleopatra may have been one of the very first to wear this fashion.

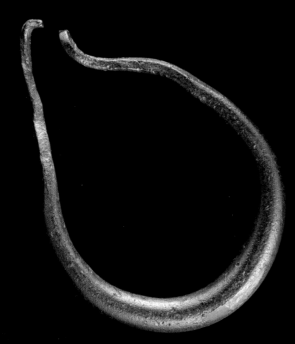

Earrings

Gold | Late Roman or Byzantine period
Diam. 1.3 cm | Th. 0.18 cm

Simple hoops with a circular cross section were used over a relatively long time period, from the Roman to the Byzantine period. This piece is one of a pair of earrings found at the site of Canopus, adding a layer of history still shrouding Egypt's mysterious last queen.

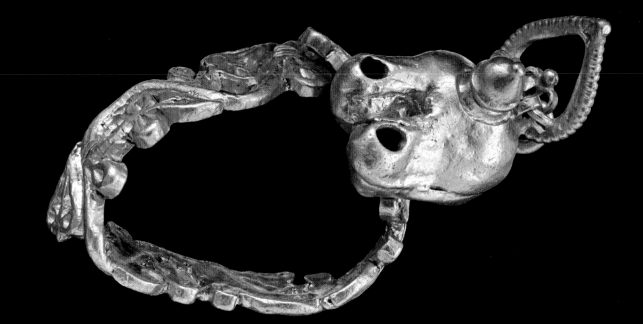

■ Ring with bezel in the form of an oil lamp

Gold | Late 6th–early 8th c. A.D.
L. 3.81 cm | W. 1.74 cm | Th. 1.08 cm

The pierced-work hoop of this one-of-a-kind ring is adorned with a wave-shaped tendril and has a bezel in the shape of an oil lamp. The lamp has two muzzles, an onion-shaped lid that hinges from the body, a drop-shaped mirror, and a handle in the shape of a simple eye.

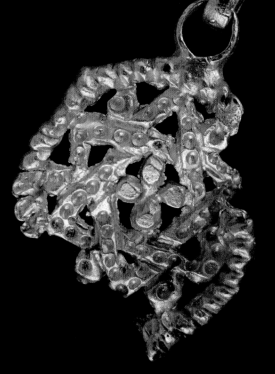

■ Chain with circular links

Gold | 6th–early 8th c. A.D.
L. 2.27 cm | W. 1.34 cm | Th. 0.14 cm

This fragmentary chain consists of a circular, pierced-work link and a smaller link or pendant. A quatrefoil ornament sits in the center of the ring, which is framed by two intertwined triangles adorned with circular punchings and an embossed cord-like frame.

CHAPTER SIX

TAPOSIRIS

THE SEARCH FOR THE TOMB of
CLEOPATRA

Zahi Hawass

Plutarch, the Roman historian, stated that Cleopatra and Mark Antony were buried together in Alexandria. For years, archaeologists believed Plutarch's conclusion. The historical evidence suggests that Cleopatra did build a tomb for herself near her royal palace, and so most scholars concluded that Cleopatra's tomb had sunk beneath the ocean floor, lost with the rest of ancient Alexandria.

Kathleen Martinez's theory, however, challenges this idea. She believes that Cleopatra and Mark Antony were buried inside the temple dedicated to Isis and Osiris at Taposiris Magna, a location about 45 kilometers west of Alexandria, near an area called Borg el Arab. The religious and political significance of the temple, along with its location, would have made this temple a logical burial place for Cleopatra, since during her reign she associated herself with Isis and Mark Antony with Osiris. The temple of Taposiris Magna was described by Plutarch as resplendent with Osirian mystery. Strabo also records that Alexander the Great stopped at this temple on his journey to the oasis at Siwa. As such, it would have been an important place to Cleopatra in life, and perhaps in death.

Cleopatra feared that in their hatred toward her, the Romans would destroy her remains. The temple of Taposiris Magna was within the ancient limits of Alexandria but outside the area controlled by the Romans, and the priests there could have easily hidden her body, keeping it safe for eternity. No other temple would have filled these needs as well, what with its religious and political significance, along with its safe location.

This structure lies between the Mediterranean Sea and Lake Mariotis, one of the 14 locations in Egypt called Abousir, where Set, according to ancient myth, scattered the pieces of Osiris's body. Ptolemy II founded the city of Taposiris Magna, but after the end of the Ptolemaic dynasty, the Romans turned the site into a fortress and dismantled the inner sanctuary. They eventually erected a church there, in the fourth century A.D., expanding it to a monastery that was abandoned at the beginning of Egypt's Arab occupation.

The first important records of the temple come from Napoleon's scientific expedition. Texts about the site were collected by scholars in this expedition but never published, although they left diagrams and maps of the site, which show that the pylons of the wall were three stories high at that time. They also provided plans of the stone tower and the crypt. Early 20th-century archaeologists found Greek inscriptions at Taposiris, including one with the names of Ptolemy II and his wife Arsinoe, the earliest found yet, along with private sanctuaries and irrigation systems around the temple.

RECENT EXCAVATIONS

Egypt's Supreme Council of Antiquities (SCA) began excavations at Taposiris in 2005. The SCA research team found many structures and artifacts in four different levels of the site, as well as shafts inside and outside the temple. In the first level, they discovered the foundations of limestone rooms built parallel to the north wall of the temple. There they recovered pottery vessels with Greek inscriptions that held oil for anointing.

Architectural components found on the second level of the temple date to the end of the Roman period. Most notable was a rectangular building consisting of three rooms, which we now know formed part of a house used by the leader of the Roman camp. Excavation on the third level revealed a five-step limestone stairway leading from the Roman house into a court.

The fourth level contained the foundations of residential houses, perhaps used by the Ptolemaic temple priests, in addition to a group of ovens and a stela inscribed in Greek. To the south of the houses, the foundation of another rectangular building contained an altar on its western end leading to the sanctuary. This building was likely a chapel dedicated to the temple gods. The arm of a marble statue of Harpocrates was found in this building, proving that all three members of the divine triad—Osiris, Isis, and Harpocrates (also known as Horus)—had a presence in the temple of Taposiris.

Researchers discovered several shafts inside and outside the temple. The first inside shaft was cut 25 meters into the rock. It contained niches used as stairs on the west and east sides. Researchers found one skeleton here and one just below it, as well as a gold collar. The excavation in this shaft continued to a depth of 35 meters, where scientists dated the sediment to the Ptolemaic period. A shaft in the southwest corner of the temple yielded a third skeleton, that of a female who died in childbirth.

Another shaft had the curious shape of a tomb entrance. The high water table prevented the research team from venturing too far down, but they did examine the debris within the shaft, discovering an alabaster head of a queen that bears a striking likeness to Cleopatra's depiction on several coins. If in fact the head is a likeness of Cleopatra, it may be the largest image of her in existence today. This is one of the most promising clues indicating that Cleopatra's tomb is at Taposiris Magna.

> "*My great-grandmother's great-grandmother was a black kitten of the sacred white cat; and the river Nile made her his seventh wife. That is why my hair is so wavy. And I always want to be let do as I like, no matter whether it is the will of the gods or not: That is because my blood is made with Nile water.*"
>
> — CLEOPATRA, in George Bernard Shaw, *Caesar and Cleopatra* (1898)

The most important discovery was a large cemetery extending to the east and west of the temple. All tombs pointed toward the temple, indicating that the cemetery was likely constructed around it. The tombs found in the cemetery fall into three categories. Chamber tombs were cut into the mountain with 13 steps down into a chamber that contained niches for burial. Pit tombs had a simple shape, containing multiple coffins cut into the mountain. Anthropoid tombs contained a single human shape; a group of these was excavated at the site, and all were found to contain remarkably preserved mummies.

Tables, lamps, and glass vessels were found near the mummies, and occasionally a layer of gold had been used to cover a mummy's open parts. A beautiful mask of gypsum with remnants of gold accompanied one young lady, and another tomb contained a hidden shaft within which lay two mummies in gold cases. Other mummies were found with hieroglyphic inscriptions on the casing. The style of the tombs and the rich variety of artifacts recovered dates this cemetery to the end of the Ptolemaic period or the beginning of the Roman period.

Another important discovery at the temple occurred during the reexcavation of the foundation of the temple's main chapel, which had been explored previously by a Hungarian expedition. A hole in the northwest corner contained three small stelae, which record that the temple was constructed during the reign of Ptolemy IV, between 221 and 205 B.C.

By following the sunset and observing the way the sun sits on the horizon of the temple pylon, researchers knew that the temple and cemetery had to be linked to one another. Some believe that the cemetery came about because the Egyptians wanted to be buried near Osiris, but the cemetery may also have been constructed for people who wanted their final resting place to be near an important person such as a king or a queen inside the temple. A radar survey of Taposiris indicated three anomalies in the rock around a depth of 25 meters, and one of these may contain the tomb of some such famous ruler. One cannot help but envision Cleopatra's tomb within that temple, and the tombs of so many of her former subjects surrounding her in a testament to her glory.

THE MYSTERY REMAINS

Until we find Cleopatra's tomb, we can only imagine the circumstances of her burial. Because there is no definitive evidence yet, archaeologists are still pursuing her tomb elsewhere, as well as among the ancient ruins of Taposiris Magna. A Greek mission working near Cleopatra's royal quarters, now underwater in Alexandria, recently raised a 9-ton tower of a pylon that is almost definitely part of the temple of Isis Lochia. They also found another exciting structure, a threshold for a monumental door that, with its red granite and copper and lead facets, may have been a part of the door to Cleopatra's tomb.

Whether or not Cleopatra was actually buried in the tomb she built for herself in Alexandria, or whether she was buried in Taposiris Magna to protect her remains from the Romans, is not yet clear. The only thing we can do is to keep looking. After years of searching, we have come a few steps closer to finding the final resting place of Cleopatra; but even when her tomb is discovered, whether deep underwater or far below the ground at Taposiris, Cleopatra will remain one of history's most mysterious, powerful, and alluring women. ∎

PAGES *198-199:* The morning sun gleams behind the Temple of Osiris at Taposiris Magna.

Small statue

Bronze | Ptolemaic period
H. 6.4 cm | W. 1.3 cm

The goddess Aphrodite stands unclothed, leaning to the left with her right leg bent. She raises her hands up to her head, holding back strands of hair that fall to her shoulders. This statue was found inside the temple wall in the northeast corner of the temple.

■ **Coin (Isis or Cleopatra)**

Bronze | Cleopatra VII (51-30 B.C.)
W. 0.2 cm | Diam. 1.7 cm

The profile on this coin seems to be Isis, or perhaps Cleopatra VII. The head is inscribed "Queen Cleopatra." This is an example of how Cleopatra portrayed herself as Isis in statues and coins.

■ **Coin (Faded Cleopatra)**

Bronze | Cleopatra VII (51-30 B.C.)
W. 0.4 cm | Diam. 2.6

Another bronze coin depicts Cleopatra's face, her hair once again tied back in a bun. On the obverse of the coin, the Ptolemaic eagle is shown with the letter Pi and a Greek inscription of Cleopatra's name.

■ **Coin**

Bronze | Cleopatra VII (51-30 B.C.)
W. 0.5 cm | Diam. 2.1 cm

Found in the chapel of the temple at Taposiris Magna, the face of Cleopatra VII looks out from this coin, her hair pulled back into her signature bun. The Greek inscription on the back reads, "Queen Cleopatra."

■ **Small coin**

Bronze | Ptolemaic period
Diam. 1.8 cm

Isis, or a queen connected with her, features prominently on the front of this coin. All coins shown here were discovered in the inner sanctuary of the temple's small chapel.

Small stela

White marble | Ptolemaic period
H. 26 cm | W. 21.5 cm | D. 6 cm

The names of Ptolemy and his wife Arsinoe, as well as the gods Serapis and Isis, are among the legible components of the inscription on this triangular stela. Parts were damaged and there is evidence of chisel marks. It was found in front of an oven to the north of the small chapel.

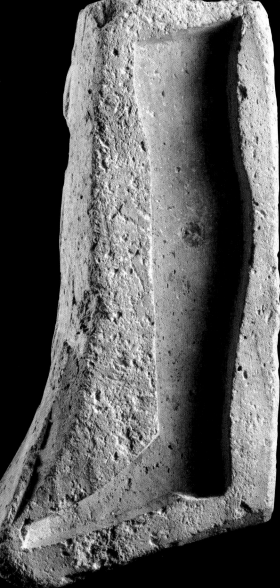

Pottery mold

Ceramic | Ptolemaic period
H. 9 cm | W. 4.6 cm | D. 1.7 cm

This small mold represents the hieroglyphic sign for the letter *b*. The mold may have been used to produce leg-shaped amulets as offerings.

▪ Small stela

Green glass | Ptolemaic period
H. 12.3 cm | W. 5.5 cm | D. 0.5 cm

Inscriptions in hieroglyphs and Greek in black cover the
ten pieces of a restored stela. Cartouches containing the
name of the king and queen appear toward the bottom.

▪ Small stela

Blue glass | Ptolemaic period
H. 11.5 cm | W. 5.7 cm | D. 0.5 cm

Broken into five pieces and mostly restored, this stela
was discovered with three others in the northwest corner
of the main temple chapel. It is inscribed with Egyptian
hieroglyphs and Greek. One cartouche in the first line reads,
"Ptolemy who lives eternally, beloved of Osiris."

The sun casts light on the archaeological dig at Taposiris.

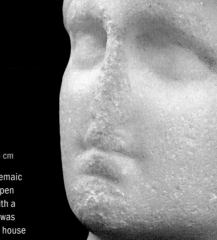

■ Statue head

Alabaster | Ptolemaic period
H. 10 cm | Diam. (head) 6.5 cm |
Diam. (neck) 3.8 cm | Circ. (neck) 5.4 cm

The beautifully sculpted face of a Ptolemaic
queen gazes straight ahead through open
eyes. The top of the head is pierced with a
hole where a crown may have gone. It was
found below the floor of the Byzantine house
in the northwestern area of the temple.

■ Head of a statue

White marble | Roman period
H. 25.5 cm | W. 21 cm | Hollow: 14 cm x 4 cm

The face of this white marble emperor is lined with wrinkles. The
eyes are defined in black, showing the remarkable features of
Alexandrian art, which often added color to statues of marble
and wood, as well as those covered with gypsum.

■ Piece of a statue

Alabaster | Ptolemaic period
L. 4.3 cm | W. 1.3 cm | D. 1.3 cm

The delicate left arm of a child, perhaps Horus, the "divine child," runs from just above the elbow to the hand, which is curled into a fist. There is a hole through the fist, indicating that it may have held an object.

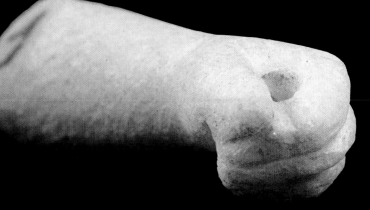

■ Piece of a statue

White marble | Ptolemaic period
L. 15 cm | W. 5 cm | Hollow: 2.8 cm x 1 cm

A beautifully carved right arm of Horus the "divine child" begins below the shoulder and ends at the fingers. The arm bends slightly at the elbow, indicating motion. The inside palm is not polished, indicating that the hand held an object.

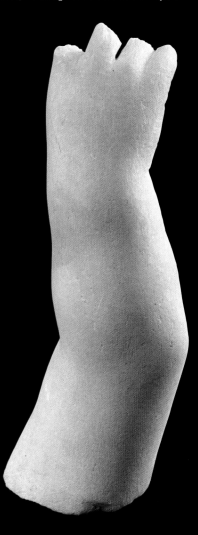

■ Part of a statue

Alabaster | Ptolemaic period
H. 8.2 cm | W. 4.6 cm | D. 3.9 cm

Found in a shaft in the southwest corner of the Osiris temple, this small human head and neck may be an image of Alexander the Great. It is not very detailed, and although the face is well defined, parts of the head and neck are missing.

Statue of a royal person

Basalt | Ptolemaic period
H. 54 cm | H. (back pillar) 40 cm |
W. (back pillar) 9 cm

The nemes headdress draping onto the shoulders
denotes the royal stature of this basalt figure. The
idealistic youthful style common in Ptolemaic royal
statuary is evident here. The hands are fisted around
short cylindrical objects, and the figure wears the
royal tripartite kilt.

Ceramic vessel

Ceramic | Late Roman period
H. 19.7 cm | W. 9 cm | W. (neck) 7 cm

A rounded body and long, narrow neck characterize the design of this pot. The body has incised lines, and an irregular red line. The vessel has been restored, and the base is rounded.

Small decorated lamp

Ceramic | Early Roman period
H. 3 cm | Diam. 7.2 cm (min.) to 8.2 cm (min.)

An image of a frog decorates this small oil lamp made of yellow clay. Oil was poured into the hole in the center and a wick inserted in the hole on the side. Soot remains can still be seen. The Greek letter alpha is stamped on the base.

■ Ceramic vessel

Ceramic | Late Roman period
H. 18.8 cm | W. (rim) 10.5 cm

The rotund body of this vessel curves inward to the wide neck, with two small handles on the sides of the high rim. The base is rounded and the body is decorated with incised lines.

■ Small ostracon

Ceramic | Ptolemaic period
L. 6 cm | W. 6 cm | D. 1 cm

Palm trees of the temple facade appear in black ink as decoration on this ostracon, or ceramic drawing surface. These markings may constitute a plan of Taposiris Magna, including a cornice of the temple with its architectural components and an inscription in Latin.

■ Lamp

Ceramic | Early Ptolemaic period
H. 5.8 cm | Diam (rim) 3 cm | Diam (wick opening) 0.8 cm

Made on a potter's wheel with handle on the rim, this lamp has a tall neck, a circular base, and a wide rim, with a hole for pouring in oil. There are remains of a black substance on the top, likely from use. A linen wick would sit inside the narrow opening.

A recent archaeological team excavates inside the temple of Taposiris Magna in search of Cleopatra's final resting place.

Vessel

Bronze | Ptolemaic period
H. 5.5 cm | L. (handle) 13.5 cm |
Diam. 19 cm

Vessels with circular, deep bowl shapes such
as this one may have been used in religious
rituals for the goddess Isis. Here, the rim
bends outward into a long, ornate handle.

■ Scale

Bronze ❘ Ptolemaic period
L. (arm) 37.5 cm ❘ Diam. (bowl) 11 cm ❘
Diam. (weight) 5.5 cm

Made of four square bronze arms, this circular
scale may have been used in spiritual rites.
A ball-shaped bronze weight accompanies the
scale, and one long piece holds a chain and
hook for suspension.

■ Lamp

Bronze ❘ Ptolemaic period
H. 3.5 cm ❘ L. (spouts) 4.5 cm ❘ Diam. (base) 4 cm

Three spouts for wicks and a wide opening in the middle
for oil contribute to the utility of this lamp's design,
which bears a likeness to those used in religious
festivals celebrating Isis, Cleopatra's chosen goddess.

■ Incense vessel

Bronze ❘ Ptolemaic period
H. 15 cm ❘ Diam. 7.2 cm

Three legs modeled after the legs of a lion
form the base of a bronze incense vessel.
The lid of this spiritual instrument is a
semicircle with decorative holes for the
incense smoke to escape.

Collar

Gold | Late Roman period
Wt. 2.23 g

Consisting of one long, thin band, this stunning collar was found recently in the course of the Taposiris excavations.

Small circle

Gold | Late Roman period
Wt. 4.4 g

This small gold piece may have once been an earring worn by a devotee who worshipped at the temple of Taposiris Magna.

Chain

Gold | Late Roman period
Wt. 3.3 g

A thin layer of gold has been molded into this rectangular shape. On the face is a decoration in the shape of a band of hair framed by two lines.

Chain

Gold | Late Roman period
Wt. 5.2 g

A thin band in rectangular shape has simple, waving lines that adorn the inner and outer faces of this gold piece.

Chain

Gold | Late Roman period
Wt. 31.5 g

Gold loops with larger links in the middle form these horseshoe-shaped chains.

Bead

Gold | Late Roman period
Wt. 4.5 g

This cylindrical bead is hollow through its length for suspension. The ends flare out, adding a dramatic flourish.

It was often difficult to discern whether the statuary produced under Cleopatra depicted the queen, the goddess Isis, or some combination of the two. The head, neck, and shoulders of the sculpture below present one such example of this dilemma. Perhaps an effort by Cleopatra to depict herself as Isis, the head is tilted slightly to the right, and the hair is styled in braids that fall to the top of the shoulders on either side of the head. The hair covers the ears in a style common in other statues of Ptolemaic queens. On the top of the head is a broken section that may be for the attachment of a crown.

The artist who sculpted this work combined humanistic beauty with the idealistic images of royalty. This statue is a model of the mixing of Egyptian and Greek elements—it is in the Hellenistic style but made of an Egyptian material, granite. The face is tilted up, the cheeks are full, and the mouth is midsize with a certain secretive smile that reminds us of the mysteries Cleopatra is still withholding from us.

■ **Part of a statue**

Granite | Ptolemaic period
H. 18.1 cm | W. 20 cm | D. 15.9 cm

The head, neck, and shoulders of this unknown woman—a Ptolemaic sculpture found during the Hungarian expedition of the 1990s, led by Győző Vörös—bear the markings of the goddess Isis.

■ Coin

Bronze | Ptolemaic period
W. 0.2 cm | Diam. 1.9 cm

A Ptolemaic king, perhaps Ptolemy IV or Alexander the Great, wears the Macedonian war crown. On the back of the coin, the Ptolemaic eagle is surrounded by the name "King Ptolemy," inscribed in Greek.

■ Coin

Bronze | Ptolemaic period
W. 0.3 cm | Diam. 2.2 cm

Likely the face of Alexander the Great wearing a crown, the Ptolemaic eagle as well as the inscription "King Ptolemy" appear on the opposite side of this coin.

■ Coin

Bronze | Ptolemaic period
W. 0.3 cm | Diam. 2.1 cm

Alexander the Great appears alongside a likeness of Zeus-Amun and the Ptolemaic eagle, as well as the inscription "King Ptolemy."

■ Coin

Bronze | Augustus (30 B.C.-A.D. 14)
W. 0.3 cm | Diam. 2.2 cm

A Roman emperor, possibly Augustus, appears on the face of this bronze coin wearing the traditional civic crown of a branch of leaves. The obverse side displays two decorative branches with three letters in the middle (not shown).

■ Coin

Bronze | Cleopatra VII (51-30 B.C.)
W. 0.4 cm | Diam. 2.1

Cleopatra's name is inscribed on the back of this coin, confirming that the face shown here is most likely that of Egypt's last Ptolemaic queen.

Archaeologist Kathleen Martinez crouches in an ancient doorway to one of many chambers in Taposiris Magna.

■ Vessel

Bronze | Ptolemaic period
H. 19 cm | Diam. (base) 8.5 cm

According to ancient writers, there was likely a great yearly festival inside the temple of Taposiris Magna. High priests in the cult of Isis would have used vessels of this style during the festival rituals to pour sacred water, while other priests would play the sistrum.

■ Lamp

Ceramic | Early Ptolemaic period
H. 4.2 cm | Diam. (rim) 3 cm | Diam. (wick opening) 0.8 cm

A potter made this lamp on a wheel, adding a handle to the rim. With a tall neck and a wide rim, it would have held ample oil, a wick inserted into the top opening. Remains of a black substance are visible on top, likely from use.

Found at Taposiris Magna, this fragment displays the nose, cheeks, mouth, and chin of an unknown man. The artist rendered the lines of the face in a realistic style, especially the cleft of the chin. The statue's surface remains smooth despite the roughness of granite as a material.

The Roman period brought the advent of new artistic styles that caused Egyptian art to evolve. The realistic features of this male face are one product of this historical shift. After carefully examining the personal features and details of this statue, archaeologists have concluded that this piece may in fact be associated with Mark Antony. Many accounts of Mark Antony note that he was handsome, often noting his cleft chin, similar to that emphasized by the artist of this work.

If Taposiris Magna proves to be the tomb of Mark Antony and Cleopatra, as we believe it to be, then this work could very well have been crafted in honor of his death.

Piece of a statue

Granite | Roman period
H. 11.8 cm | W. 10.1 cm | D. 9 cm

The face depicted in this piece of a statue, found during Vörös's Hungarian expedition as well, may be that of Mark Antony.

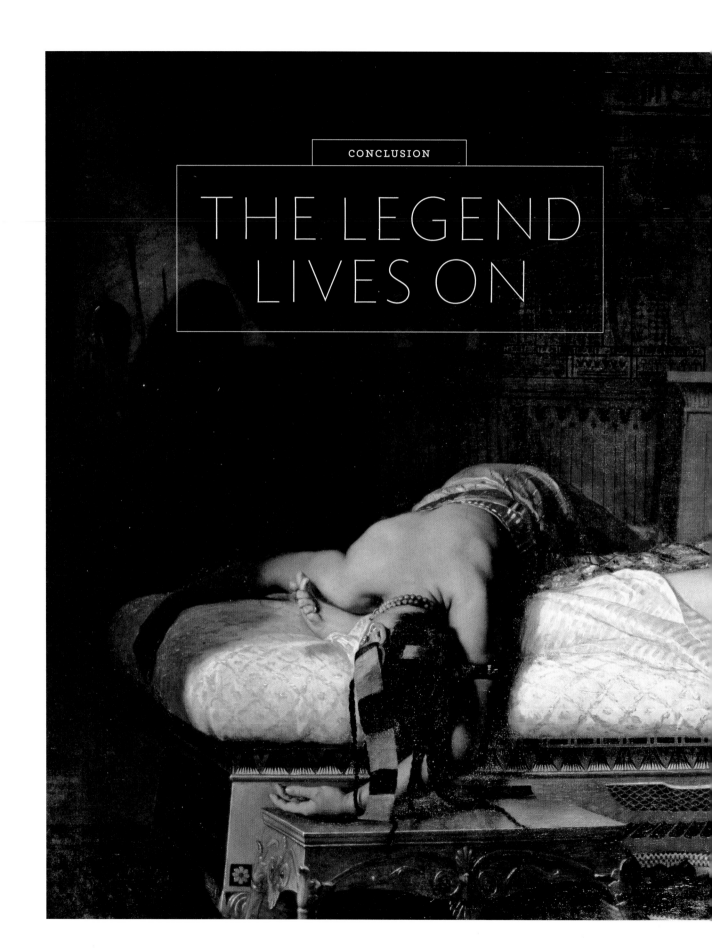

THE LEGEND LIVES ON

QUEEN of HISTORY & MYSTERY

Zahi Hawass

No other queen of the ancient world—not Hatshepsut or Nefertiti, not Helen of Troy or Boudicca of the Celts—carries with her the intrigue of Egypt's Queen Cleopatra VII. Her life, her politics, and her romantic encounters have given her a magical appeal that has captivated the world ever since. Over the years, her tale has been told and retold, and often reinterpreted; her image has been reinvented by age after age in light of each succeeding style of art and fashion. And still the story of Cleopatra remains rich, ruthless, and alluring.

And to think that this is a woman whose appearance we cannot even know for certain. Years ago, a British Museum curator examined the royal statues of the queen and the coins stamped with her image and stated that her face was not what one would consider beautiful by modern standards. Reports that the queen was fat, frumpy, and had a large hooked nose, bad teeth, sharp eyes, and a fat-folded neck, spread throughout the press. "Ancient Coin Suggests Cleopatra Was No Beauty," read the headlines. And yet we continue to be fascinated by this woman who made history.

Those who came after her—in particular Augustus Caesar and the Roman officials who took over rule in Egypt after her death—deliberately did all they could to destroy any images of her, as if to destroy them was to obliterate her power and reputation. Yet still the remarkable story of this Ptolemaic queen, Egypt's last pharaoh, has come down through history. As 17th-century French philosopher Blaise Pascal wrote, "Cleopatra's nose: If it had been shorter, the whole face of the earth would have been different."

Beautiful or not by today's standards, this queen captured the hearts of the two most powerful men of her time, and her story has fascinated countless historians, writers, and artists.

PREVIOUS PAGES: Jean André Rixens, French painter of the 19th century, envisioned the scene of Cleopatra's death, one handmaiden dying with her and the other still on guard.

OPPOSITE: Michelangelo interpreted Cleopatra's beauty with full lips and a round face, an asp wrapped around her neck.

PLUTARCH'S *LIFE*

The earliest version of Cleopatra's story, written by Plutarch around A.D. 100 in his *Lives of Noble Grecians and Romans*, contains accounts considered to be the most accurate and complete—and here the myth begins. In narrating the life of Mark Antony, Plutarch calls the Roman leader's love affair with Cleopatra "the last and crowning mischief that could befall him" and emphasizes her seductive charms. According to Plutarch, knowing she was to meet Mark Antony, the Egyptian queen came sailing up the river Cydnus, in a barge with gilded stern and outspread sails of purple, while oars of silver beat time to

the music of flutes and fifes and harps. She lay all alone under a canopy of cloth of gold, dressed as Venus in a painting, and beautiful young boys, like painted Cupids, stood on each side to fan her. Her maids were dressed like sea nymphs and graces, some steering at the rudder, some working at the ropes.

There follows an extravagant courtship, together with a characterization of Cleopatra not as beautiful but as intelligent and bewitching, so much so that Antony neglected his civic duties at home. "While Fulvia his wife maintained his quarrels in Rome against Octavius Caesar by actual force of

In "The Visit of Cleopatra to Antony," Italian Renaissance painter de' Landi depicted crowds in Tarsus, awaiting the barge with Egypt's queen.

arms," Antony allowed himself "to be carried away by her to Alexandria, there to keep holiday, like a boy, in play and diversion." Plutarch quotes a friend of his own grandfather's as to the sumptuousness of the feasts they shared.

It is from Plutarch as well that we hear the earliest version of the intertwined death of Mark Antony and Cleopatra. Making one bad decision after another, and falling under the shadow of numerous omens reflecting the gods' ill will, Mark Antony decides to die a soldier's death. He witnesses his own men surrendering to Octavius, his Roman rival, and blames Cleopatra. "She, being afraid lest in his fury and despair he might do her a mischief, fled to her monument," writes Plutarch, and "sent messengers who should tell Antony she was dead." Believing himself defeated in war and love, Antony wounds himself with his sword but lives long enough to be brought before Cleopatra.

"Nothing could part us whilst we lived, but death seems to threaten to divide us," Plutarch reports that Cleopatra said upon Antony's death. The passionate queen had already spent days testing various poisons, watching prisoners die "in order to see which of them were the least painful in the operation." Refusing to allow the Romans to take her prisoner back to Rome, she selected the most painless—the bite of an asp—although of her mode of suicide, even Plutarch admits a lack of sure knowledge. Perhaps an asp brought in a basket of figs; perhaps a golden spindle holding poison: Whatever her actual mode of suicide, in the triumphant procession organized by Octavius after her death, "there was carried a figure of Cleopatra, with an asp clinging to her," and the story was confirmed. The figure portrayed her respectfully, according to Plutarch, since the Romans "could not but admire the greatness of her spirit, and gave order that her body should be buried by Antony with royal splendor and magnificence."

Hathor, god of love and motherhood, Ptolemy XVI Caesarion, son of Julius Caesar and Cleopatra, and Cleopatra herself are engraved on the outer wall of the Hathor temple at Dendera, built late in the Ptolemaic dynasty.

OPPOSITE: In this 1888 painting by John William Waterhouse entitled "Cleopatra," the queen sits draped in white, an intricate golden crown atop her head. With her lips flushed and her eyes intent, Cleopatra is at the height of power and seduction.

All the material was there, in Plutarch's version, whether fact in whole or in part, and yet open enough to interpretation that poets, dramatists, artists, and filmmakers had plenty of room to retell the story for their own times. The 14th-century story-teller Geoffrey Chaucer, best known for *The Canterbury Tales*, included Cleopatra's tale among his *Legends of Good Women*, a tongue-in-cheek set of stories intended to put women in a good light. "And she hir deeth receyveth, with good chere," he wrote, "for love of Antony, that was hir so dere."

A little more than a century later, perhaps the most influential retelling ever was conceived: William Shakespeare's *Antony and Cleopatra*, written and first performed in the first decade of the 17th century. Shakespeare's tragedy captures the complicated nature both of the Egyptian queen's character and the passions that overtook her and the Roman general who died by her side. Considered one of Shakespeare's great tragedies, *Antony and Cleopatra* has been performed through the centuries, in many languages, and around the world, on stage and more recently on film and television—surely one of the reasons that the story of Cleopatra has stayed alive in the world's collective imagination.

The English poet and playwright John Dryden, who greatly admired Shakespeare's play, wrote his own version of the tragic ending of Cleopatra's life in the play *All for Love, or The World Well Lost*, first performed in 1678.

A garnet wire pendant dating to the second or third century B.C. is framed below and above by blossom-shaped gold sheets.

OPPOSITE: Helen Hayes takes a girlish pose as Cleopatra in George Bernard Shaw's *Caesar and Cleopatra*, around 1925.

IMAGES OF CLEOPATRA

Visual artists, as well as poets and dramatists, have found inspiration in the fascinating character of Cleopatra through the ages. Portraits often play upon the striking contrast between her erotic charms and her method of suicide, playing up the symbolism of the serpent and entwining images of femininity and eroticism with those of death and evil. Michelangelo himself sketched her, Medusa-like, with snakes entwining her twisted hair. Baroque painters like Giovanni Francesco Barbieri and Artemisia Gentileschi—the first female painter accepted into the Accademia di Arte del Disegno in Florence, Italy—both created paintings of Cleopatra's death, emphasizing the drama, suffering, and eroticism of the scene.

Cleopatra tests poisons on Egyptian prisoners in preparation for her own death in Alexandre Cabanel's 1887 work.

French artists of the 19th century, fascinated by the Orient, envisaged Cleopatra as a symbol of that other world. Whether portrayed as a temptress—as in the 1866 painting by Jean-Léon Gérôme, "Cléopatre et César," showing the queen emerging from a sumptuous Persian carpet and entrancing Caesar—or a ruthless autocrat—as in the 1887 painting by Alexandre Cabanel, "Cleopatra Testing Poisons on Condemned Prisoners"—she represented a mysterious and powerful being from a far-off land. Jean-André Rixens captured the same mystery and exoticism in his painting "Death of Cleopatra" (1874).

Each new school of painters evoked their own interpretation of the queen. For the late 19th-century Pre-Raphaelites, Cleopatra had emigrated into the realm of myth and goddesses. John William Waterhouse, influenced by the Pre-Raphaelites who preceded him, painted an auburn-haired, brooding Queen Cleopatra, abstracting her from any specific scene in her dramatic life story and concentrating on character instead.

ON THE SILVER SCREEN

Film was in its infancy when Cleopatra first appeared on the silver screen in a two-minute silent film, *Cléopâtre*, created by the French filmmaking pioneer Georges Méliès in 1899. A longer silent film produced in 1908, based on Shakespeare's *Antony and Cleopatra*, starred Florence Lawrence. Generation after generation, the legend of Cleopatra inspired some of the most sumptuous extravaganzas ever created by Hollywood. Actress Theda Bara portrayed the Egyptian queen in a 1917 silent film; posters and still photos show her intricate costumes—so revealing that later film censors banned the film—but no prints of the entire film survive today. Cecil B. DeMille's 1934 film starred Claudette Colbert as Cleopatra in another spectacular, and expensive, production.

Russian ballerina Lubov Tchernicheva danced the role of Cleopatra in a ballet choreographed by George Balanchine in the 1920s.

OPPOSITE: The iconic 20th-century Hollywood Cleopatra, Elizabeth Taylor starred with Richard Burton as Mark Antony in the 1963 film.

In 1963 Joseph L. Mankiewicz directed the landmark 20th-Century Fox production of *Cleopatra*, starring Elizabeth Taylor, Richard Burton, and Rex Harrison. More than three hours long—in fact, divided into two parts, with an intermission between them—the film won four Oscars and cost about $44 million to produce, a staggering sum in those days.

In 1990, a Pakistani production entitled *Miss Cleopatra,* starring Babra Sharif and directed by Javed Fazil, positioned the story in present-day Pakistan. After a woman awakens the spirit of Mark Antony, he starts to stalk her, believing her to be his long-lost queen. Television scriptwriters have also reveled in the legends of Cleopatra, creating spectacles for the world to see, such as the eight-part BBC drama series entitled *The Cleopatras,* which aired in 1983 and dramatized the lives of all the Ptolemaic queens named Cleopatra.

WHO WAS CLEOPATRA?

In every medium, for hundreds of years, artists have taken pleasure in evoking the mythic power of Cleopatra. They have told the story again and again of this beautiful, powerful, and intelligent woman whose life was filled with conflict and triumph, passion and tragedy, and whose fate entwined with some of the most powerful men not just of her day but of all time. What is it that continues to fascinate us about this woman?

Is it her beauty? Strangely enough, we have little evidence that shows what she really looked like, and what little we have—the few coins on which we believe her profile is sculpted—suggest a face that does not conform to conventional notions of female beauty.

Is it her power? We admire a woman who holds her own among world leaders and military generals, as Cleopatra did. And yet Cleopatra's rule marked the endpoint of the Ptolemaic dynasty. Hers was the last reign by a pharaoh, a legacy that reached back thousands of years but came to an end with her death.

Is it her intelligence? We learn from ancient sources that she was educated, knowledgeable, and sophisticated, and we gather from stories about her that she was clever to the point of being cunning.

Beauty, power, intelligence—all three contribute to the everlasting legend. But at the heart of her intrigue is mystery itself. We know less about Cleopatra than we do about many other figures through history, and yet we are drawn into her spell, seeking always to understand and know more, just as those who knew her in person seem to have been.

And so, in the waters and desert of Egypt, the search for Cleopatra goes on. ∎

THE EXHIBITION

John Norman PRESIDENT *ARTS AND EXHIBITIONS INTERNATIONAL*

Early in 2008, my business partner Andy Numhauser and I faced a task: to come up with a new exhibition concept for Arts and Exhibitions International. We knew the topic had to be spectacular and yet easily grasped by everyone. As we carried out our research, the name "Cleopatra" kept coming up. One of the most popular and enigmatic characters of all time, she led a life full of mystery, power, love, romance, intrigue, glamour, tragedy, and violence—all the makings of a great story and ultimately a great exhibition. Even though Cleopatra's charm, intelligence, and beauty are legendary, it's hard to separate fact from legend. She is one of the best known historical figures, but no one knows for sure what she really looked like. It is no wonder that this mysterious character has been the subject of dozens of movies. What we needed were the artifacts through which we could tell her story. But no one has found her tomb, and so finding such artifacts seemed unlikely.

Then I learned about the underwater excavations of Franck Goddio—and suddenly the project took off.

I met with Franck in Bonn, Germany, at the exhibition "Egypt's Sunken Treasures." Immediately I knew that the two of us were going to become good friends. Franck has decades of experience in underwater archaeology, and his expertise in the physical landscape of ancient Alexandria and the surrounding area is unparalleled. Years of research and exploration have led to the recovery of hundreds of artifacts from the Bay of Aboukir—the ancient port of Alexandria—as well as from the lost cities of Canopus and Heracleion, both submerged for centuries and practically forgotten. At Alexandria, Franck discovered Cleopatra's own palace, temples built during her reign, and objects that she herself may have used. Over the next few months, we developed an exhibition theme that incorporated many of Franck's discoveries. Using these objects, never before seen in the United States, we could integrate the ancient tales of Cleopatra with a modern account of Franck's groundbreaking work.

Our next step was to put together the creative team to develop the story line, design the exhibition elements, and create a fresh, new presentation. People today use technology in very sophisticated ways—almost everyone receives information via smartphones or computers. Determined to take advantage of this trend, we set out to design an experience for the contemporary visitor. Using high-definition footage from Franck's work in Egypt, we could deliver our content visually, using video displays to tell our story.

As the project moved ahead, we hired Tom Fricker as the designer and Sharon Simpson as the writer of the exhibition. After working together with this same team on several successful exhibitions in the past, we were confident they could deliver the results we sought. We also decided to enlist the National Geographic Society as our partner. With an international reputation, long experience in underwater archaeology, and expertise in designing exhibition catalogs, NGS was the right match for our project. Together with our Arts and Exhibitions production team, we started on the development phase.

While researching content for the exhibition, we learned of Dr. Zahi Hawass and Dr. Kathleen Martinez's work at the ancient site of Taposiris Magna, west of Alexandria, searching for the tomb of Cleopatra and Mark Antony. At his invitation, Andy and I visited him at the site, where we learned about the history of this ancient temple and examined the physical evidence that has convinced Dr. Hawass that he has found the final resting place of Cleopatra and her lover. We watched as several workers meticulously dug through the sand, patiently looking for artifacts and clues. We were so impressed by this ongoing effort that we decided to incorporate Dr. Hawass's work into the last section of the exhibition.

Finally we had all the pieces in place to organize a world-class exhibition. The captivating story of Cleopatra would unfold through objects that she had actually seen, built, or touched, and we would tell it alongside the contemporary story of the search by our two modern-day explorers for more information about this enigmatic and legendary queen.

"Cleopatra: The Search for the Last Queen of Egypt" is truly a collaboration by many individuals. I would like to thank each of the people who has worked on the project. I would also like to thank AEG Live and Phil Anschutz for believing in this exhibition, for their continued support of our efforts, and for allowing us to bring this fascinating story to the public.

None of this would be possible without the support of Dr. Zahi Hawass, Vice Minister of Culture of Egypt and Secretary General of the Supreme Council of Antiquities, whom we thank for his trust and continued support.

ACKNOWLEDGMENTS

Franck Goddio, president of the Institut Européen d'Archéologie Sous-Marine (IEASM) and director of the excavations, would like to thank all those who have contributed to the success of the excavations in Egypt:

IN THE ARAB REPUBLIC OF EGYPT

Farouk Hosni, *Minister of Culture of Egypt*
Zahi Hawass, *Secretary General of the Supreme Council of Antiquities*

SUPREME COUNCIL OF ANTIQUITIES OF EGYPT

General Samah Kchtab, *Financial Director*
Sabri Abd el-Aziz, *General Director of Egyptian Archaeology*
Mohamed Abd el-Maksoud, *Director of Egyptian Archaeology*
Mohamed Abd el-Fatah, *General Director of the Museums of Egypt*
Mohamed Ismaïl, *Director of the Foreign Archaeological Mission*
Ibrahim A. Darwish, *General Director of the Museums of Alexandria*

Egyptian Museum, *Cairo*
Wafaa el-Saddik, *Director, Egyptian Museum, Department of Exhibitions Abroad*
Albert Ghaly, *Egyptian Museum, Department of Exhibitions Abroad*
Lotfi Abd el-Hamid, *Egyptian Museum, Department of Exhibitions Abroad*

Maritime Museum, *Alexandria*
Greco-Roman Museum, *Alexandria*
National Museum, *Alexandria*
Bibliotheca Alexandrina
University of Alexandria

SPECIAL THANKS to the Egyptian Coast Guard and the Egyptian Navy, responsible for the maritime area in which the mission has taken place.

THE SUPREME COUNCIL OF ANTIQUITIES (SCA) assists the government of Egypt in its decisions concerning Egyptian cultural heritage and is the supervising authority for the Ministry of Culture's responsibilities regarding Pharaonic, Islamic, Coptic, and other historical sites and monuments. The SCA plans and implements antiquities policy and coordinates the activities of its cultural heritage committees. It issues resolutions on and guidelines for the study and protection of antiquities, as well as encourages and manages archaeological research and museums. It oversees the publication of works on the study of art and civilization, and it finances archaeological excavations and conservation projects. The SCA's mission is to promote historical culture, both on its own and in cooperation with national and international organizations.

THIS PROJECT WOULD NOT HAVE BEEN POSSIBLE without the passionate work of all the participants in the various missions in Egypt, the collaboration and support of the Supreme Council of Antiquities, and the knowledge and advice of the scientists who have supported us.

INSTITUT EUROPÉEN D'ARCHÉOLOGIE SOUS-MARINE

Amani Badr | Alexander Belov | Olivier Berger | Jean-Paul Blancan | Georges Brocot | Stéphane Brousse | Bernard Camier | Guy de Castéja | Jean Castéra | Jonathan Cole | Tatiana Curchod | Grégory Dalex | Jérôme Delafosse | Alain Denaix | David Fabre | Michael Fitzgerald | Mohamed Mahmoud Galal | Patrick Gay | Christoph Gerigk | Catherine Grataloup | Jean-Jacques Groussard | Antoine Guillain | Susan Hendrickson | Ghislaine d'Antras de Jourdan | Lionel Julien | Sophie Lalbat | Gildas Lesouef | Zizi Louxor | Arnel Manalo | Henri-Bernard Maugiron | Mahmoud Mohammed Aly | Pascal Morisset | Bobby Orillaneda | Frédéric Osada | Rosario Palacios Calleya | Laurent Pellemoine | Fernando Pereira | Alain Peton | Nicolas Ponzone | Michel Revest | Pablo Rodríguez | Alejandra de Rojas | Jean-Claude Roubaud | Philippe Rousseau | Arnaud Roy | Patrice Sandrin | Roland Savoye | Gérard Schnepp | Eric Smith | Keith Smith | Yann Streiff | Jean-Louis de Talancé | Emily Teeter | Daniel Visnikar

SUPPORTING RESEARCHERS

Sally-Ann Ashton, *Senior Assistant Keeper, The Fitzwilliam Museum, Cambridge* | **Kim Ayodeji,** *Archaeologist, Institute of Classical Studies, London* | **John Baines,** *Professor of Egyptology, University of Oxford* | **Salwa Hussein Bakr,** *Egyptologist, Tanta University* | **Olivier Berger,** *Conservator and Restorer, Museum of Archaeology, Basel* | **Étienne Bernand,** *Honorary Professor, Collège de France, Paris* | **A. Sophie von Bomhard,** *Paris* | **Cécile Bresc,** *British Museum, London* | **Manfred Clauss,** *Professor of Ancient History, Free University of Berlin* | **Zoe Cox,** *Institute of Archaeology, University of Oxford* | **Françoise Dunand,** *Professor, Faculty of Social and Human Sciences, University of Strasburg* | **David Fabre,** *Egyptologist, Paris* | **Catherine Grataloup,** *Ceramologist, Lyon* | **Tom Hardwick,** *Keeper of Egyptology and Archaeology, Bolton Museum and Art Gallery* | **Amira Abou Bakr el-Khoust,** *Head Curator, Supreme Council of Antiquities, Alexandria and Marsa Matruh* | **Zsolt Kiss,** *Centre for Mediterranean Archaeology, Warsaw* | **Emma Libonati,** *Laycock Scholar in Egyptology, Worcester College, University of Oxford* | **Barbara Lichocka,** *Centre for Mediterranean Archaeology, Warsaw* | **Eric McCann,** *Egyptologist, Institute of Archaeology, University College, London* | **Andrew Meadows,** *Margaret Thompson Curator of Greek Coins, American Numismatic Society, London* | **Cécile Morrisson,** *Centre National de la Recherche Scientifique, Collège de France, Paris* | **Claire Piffaut,** *Restorer of Stone, Bari* | **Ashraf Abdel-Raouf Ragheb,** *Egyptologist, Supreme Council of Antiquities, Alexandriai* | **Nicholas Victor Sekunda,** *Professor of Archaeology, Gdansk University* | **R. R. R. Smith,** *Lincoln Professor of Classical Archaeology and Art, University of Oxford* | **Yvonne Stolz,** *Research Centre for Anatolian Civilisations, Koç University, Istanbul* | **Luc Tamborero,** *Stonecutter, Bari* | **Michel Tardieu,** *Collège de France, Paris* | **Christophe Thiers,** *Egyptologist, Centre National de la Recherche Scientifique, Montpellier* | **Susan Walker,** *Keeper of Greek and Roman Antiquities, The Ashmolean Museum, Oxford* | **Ahmed Abd el-Fattah Youssef,** *former Director of the Museums of Alexandria* | **Jean Yoyotte,** *Egyptologist, Honorary Professor, Collège de France, Paris*

IN FRANCE

French Embassy in Egypt
General Consulate of France in Alexandria
Ministry of Foreign Affairs, *General Directorate for Cooperation, Development, and Francophony*

HILTI FOUNDATION

Georg Rosenbauer, *Hilti Foundation*
Hans Saxer, *Hilti Foundation*
Dieter A. Irion, Daniela Bühe, Katrin Wollgast, *Salaction Public Relations*
Roland Savoye, Pascal Morisset, *Cinematography*
Christoph Gerigk assisted by Sonja Dräger, Gülten Hamidanoglu, *Photography*
Olivier Berger, *Coordinator of Conservation and Restoration and his team*
Alberto de Gil Ricard, Gregor Lersch, *Technical Assistance*
Nadine Eichenberger, Ines Kausch, Sophie Lalbat, Andrea Mähr, *Coordination & Support*
Leah Kelso, *Coordination, Hilti North America*

SPECIAL THANKS to the Hilti Foundation for its generous support of the continuing work of IEASM and for its contributions to this exhibition and the accompanying book.

THE HILTI FOUNDATION   HILTI FOUNDATION

THE FASCINATION OF HISTORY—researching the past, making new discoveries, presenting findings to the public—these are the goals shared by Franck Goddio and the Hilti Foundation (*www.hilti-foundation.org*).

The Martin Hilti Family Trust is the sole shareholder of the globally operating Hilti Group. Hilti provides state-of-the-art technological products, systems, and services for the construction industry. Close to 20,000 employees in more than 120 countries are passionately committed to exceeding customer expectations and to building a better future. Hilti Group was founded in Liechtenstein in 1941, and the headquarters of both the Hilti Group and the Hilti Foundation are based in Schaan in the Principality of Liechtenstein. Out of the 20,000 employees, 1,800 work at the Liechtenstein headquarters.

Established in 1996 by the Martin Hilti Family Trust, the Hilti Foundation finances and coordinates all global corporate social responsibility activities on behalf of the Hilti Group and the Trust. The Hilti Foundation is committed to a select range of innovative and sustainable projects, particularly in the cultural, social, and educational domain. Just as the Hilti logo has long been recognized as the hallmark of innovative products and market services, the name Hilti Foundation stands for the promotion of innovative ideas and projects that contribute to building a better future, as put forth in the Hilti mission statement.

Since 1996, the focus of the Hilti Foundation's cultural commitment has been the support of underwater archaeological work off the Egyptian coast by Franck Goddio and his team. Franck Goddio works closely with renowned experts and scientists and enjoys the scientific support of the Centre for Maritime Archaeology at the University of Oxford in Oxford, U.K.

The current exhibition presents to a broad public audience the spectacular finds and results of Franck Goddio's painstaking research.

INSTITUT EUROPÉEN D'ARCHÉOLOGIE SOUS-MARINE

FOUNDED BY FRANCK GODDIO IN 1985, the Institut Européen d'Archéologie Sous-Marine (IEASM) is a nonprofit organization dedicated to the location, exploration, study, and restoration of sunken sites and to the presentation of their treasures. The artifacts from Canopus, Heracleion, and Alexandria shown in this exhibition are the result of sophisticated research and exploration methods by IEASM. The realization of this exhibition has been supported by the IEASM.

I.E.A.S.M

FURTHER ACKNOWLEDGMENTS

John Baines, *Professor of Egyptology, University of Oxford*
André Bernand, *Professor Emeritus*
Étienne Bernand, *Professor Emeritus*
Barry Cunliffe, *Professor Emeritus of European Archaeology, University of Oxford*
Florence Gould Foundation
Chris Gosden, *Professor of European Archaeology, University of Oxford*
Damian Robinson, *Director, Oxford Centre for Maritime Archaeology (OCMA), University of Oxford*
R. R. R. Smith, *Lincoln Professor of Classical Archaeology and Art, University of Oxford*
Andrew Wilson, *Professor of Roman Archaeology, University of Oxford*
Jean Yoyotte, *Honorary Professor of the Collège de France*

ARTS AND EXHIBITIONS INTERNATIONAL an AEG Live Company

John Norman, *President, Executive Producer*
Andres Numhauser, *Executive Vice President*
Michael Sampliner, *Chief Operating Officer*
Mark Lach, *Senior Vice President*
Bryan Harris, *Vice President, Sales and Marketing*
Natasha Badgerow, *Senior Project Manager*
Chantelle Blayney, *Project Manager*
Kristina Robbins, *Project Manager*
Jason Simmons, *General Manager*
Jeff Wyatt, *Vice President, Project Management*
Laura Calliari, *Senior Director, Public Relations*
Chris Jacobs, *Marketing Manager*
Arbana Dollani, *Assistant Project Manager*

Katie Lynn Beach, *Director of Ticket Operations*
Jennifer LaRock, *Manager of Ticket Operations*
Garrett Miller, *Regional Controller*
Bernadett Swarthout, *Accounting*
Marcia Marshall, *Accounts Payable*
Jessica Baynard, *Staff Accountant*
Jolie Kass, *Director of Exhibition Operations*
Jaclyn Pyatt, *General Manager*
Michael Pyatt, *Asst. General Manager*
Gemma Levett, *General Manager*
Beth Crawford, *Asst. General Manager*
Richard Bright, *Production Manager*

CONTENT, DESIGN, AND INSTALLATION

Sharon Simpson, SJS Projects, Inc., *Exhibition Writer*
Tom Fricker, Fricker Studio, *Exhibition Designer*
P. David Silverman, *Guest Curator*
David Dailing, *Artifact Supervisor*
David Carone, *Registrar*
Allan Sprecher, *Artifact Installation*
Atlantic Productions, *Media Production*
Margaret B. Stogner, Blue Bear Films, *Media Production*
Darryl Kinson, *Media Production*

Kenneth L. Garrett, *Photography*
David Mauk, *Music Composition*
Sam Rembert, *Lighting Production*
Heather Watson, Eileen Hiraike, Hunt Design, *Graphic Design*
Moss Communications, *Scenic Fabric & Imagery Production*
Crush Creative, *Graphic Production*
Design Electronics, *Audio/Visual*
Benosh Productions, *Display Production*
Lexington Studios, *Exhibition Production*

NATIONAL GEOGRAPHIC SOCIETY

Terry Garcia, *Executive Vice President, Mission Programs*
Sarah Laskin, *Vice President, Mission Programs*
Kathryn Keane, *Director, Traveling Exhibitions Development*
Mimi Koumanelis, *Vice President, Communications*
Cindy Beidel, *Communications*

FURTHER READING

ANCIENT SOURCES & LITERARY APPEARANCES

Plutarch, *Lives of the Noble Greeks and Romans* (late 1st century A.D.). An essential classical source for the biographies of many ancients. Cleopatra appears in the lives of Julius Caesar and Mark Antony.

Dio Cassius, *Roman History* (ca A.D. 230). The surviving fragments of this massive history of Rome, written in Greek by a third-century Roman consul, include the story of Mark Antony and Cleopatra.

Geoffrey Chaucer, *The Legend of Good Women* (1381). Chaucer's tongue-in-cheek poem about feminine virtue includes Cleopatra among sirens and tragic women of myth and ancient history.

William Shakespeare, *Antony and Cleopatra* (1606). Shakespeare based entire passages of this play, one of his last tragedies, on a 1579 English translation of Plutarch's *Lives*.

Sir Thomas Browne, *Pseudodoxia Epidemica* (1672). The English philosopher discusses how Cleopatra committed suicide, comparing historic fact with artistic portrayals through the centuries.

John Dryden, *All for Love, or the World Well Lost* (1677). Restoration England's arbiter of taste demonstrated his definition of tragedy by writing Cleopatra's story in heroic couplets.

Sarah Fielding, *The Lives of Cleopatra and Octavia* (1757). This early English novelist—sister to Henry Fielding, author of *Tom Jones*—wrote the life stories of Mark Antony's wife and lover.

H. Rider Haggard, *Cleopatra* (1889). The Victorian romance novelist imagines the discovery of an ancient papyrus that tells Cleopatra's story through the eyes of a priest of Osiris.

George Bernard Shaw, *Caesar and Cleopatra* (1898). The popular English playwright dramatized Cleopatra's relationship with Julius Caesar, including her appearance before him, unrolled from inside a carpet.

MODERN WORKS

Michel Chauveau, *Egypt in the Age of Cleopatra* (Cornell University Press, 2000).

——, *Cleopatra : Beyond the Myth* (Cornell University Press, 2002).

Franck Goddio, David Fabre, ed., *Egypt's Sunken Treasures,* 2nd ed. (Prestel, 2008).

Prudence Jones, *Cleopatra: The Last Pharaoh* (American University in Cairo Press, 2006).

Joyce Tyldesley, *Cleopatra: Last Queen of Egypt* (Profile Books, 2008).

FOR CHILDREN

Laura Foreman and Franck Goddio, *Cleopatra's Palace: In Search of a Legend* (Discovery Channel, 1999).

Diane Stanley, *Cleopatra* (HarperCollins, 1997).

ILLUSTRATION CREDITS

All images by Christoph Gerigk unless otherwise noted.

Kenneth Garrett: 1; 6-7; 22-23; 27 (LO); 47; 50; 51; 53; 67; 76; 77; 106; 107; 113; 140; 145; 146 (UP); 148; 152; 165 (D); 167; 179; 198-199; 204 (LE); 204 (RT); 205 (UP LE); 205 (UP RT); 205 (LO LE); 205 (LO RT); 206 (UP); 206 (RT); 207 (up); 207 (LO); 208-209; 210 (UP); 210 (LO); 211 (UP); 211 (LE); 211 (RT); 212; 213; 214 (UP); 214 (LO); 215 (UP); 215 (CTR); 215 (LO); 216-217; 218; 219 (UP); 219 (CTR); 219 (LO); 220 (UP); 220 (CTR); 220 (LO); 221 (UP); 221 (CTR); 221 (LO); 222; 223 (A); 223 (B); 223 (C); 223 (D); 223 (E); 224-225; 226 (LE); 226 (RT); 227.

16, HIP/Art Resource, NY; 27 (B), Erich Lessing/Art Resource, NY; 27 (C), DeA Picture Library/Art Resource, NY; 27 (D), Sandro Vannini; 27 (E), Sandro Vannini; 27 (F), Bildarchiv Preussischer Kulturbesitz/Art Resource, NY; 27 (G), Réunion des Musées Nationaux/Art Resource, NY; 150-151, Jérôme Delafosse; 186, Reuters/CORBIS; 187, Reuters/CORBIS; 228-229, Imagno/Getty Images; 231, Art Resource, NY; 232-233, North Carolina Museum of Art/CORBIS; 234, The Bridgeman Art Library; 235, Erich Lessing/Art Resource, NY; 236, Conde Naste Archive/CORBIS; 238-239, Christie's Images/CORBIS; 240, E.O. Hoppe/CORBIS; 241, Bettmann/CORBIS; 243, Bettmann/CORBIS.

INDEX

CLEOPATRA: THE SEARCH FOR THE LAST QUEEN OF EGYPT
BY ZAHI HAWASS & FRANCK GODDIO

PUBLISHED BY THE NATIONAL GEOGRAPHIC SOCIETY

JOHN M. FAHEY, JR., *President and Chief Executive Officer*

GILBERT M. GROSVENOR, *Chairman of the Board*

TIM T. KELLY, *President, Global Media Group*

JOHN Q. GRIFFIN, *Executive Vice President; President, Publishing*

NINA D. HOFFMAN, *Executive Vice President; President, Book Publishing Group*

PREPARED BY THE BOOK DIVISION

BARBARA BROWNELL GROGAN, *Vice President and Editor in Chief*

MARIANNE R. KOSZORUS, *Director of Design*

CARL MEHLER, *Director of Maps*

R. GARY COLBERT, *Production Director*

JENNIFER A. THORNTON, *Managing Editor*

MEREDITH C. WILCOX, *Administrative Director, Illustrations*

STAFF FOR THIS BOOK

SUSAN TYLER HITCHCOCK, *Project Editor*

SANAA AKKACH, *Art Director*

DANA CHIVVIS, *Illustrations Editor*

JESSICA RIGHTHAND, *Assistant Project Editor*

LISA A. WALKER, *Production Project Manager*

ROBERT WAYMOUTH, *Illustrations Specialist*

AL MORROW, *Design Assistant*

ALLISON GAFFNEY, *Design Intern*

MANUFACTURING AND QUALITY MANAGEMENT

CHRISTOPHER A. LIEDEL, *Chief Financial Officer*

PHILLIP L. SCHLOSSER, *Vice President*

CHRIS BROWN, *Technical Director*

NICOLE ELLIOTT, *Manager*

RACHEL FAULISE, *Manager*

The National Geographic Society is one of the world's largest nonprofit scientific and educational organizations. Founded in 1888 to "increase and diffuse geographic knowledge," the Society works to inspire people to care about the planet. It reaches more than 325 million people worldwide each month through its official journal, *National Geographic,* and other magazines; National Geographic Channel; television documentaries; music; radio; films; books; DVDs; maps; exhibitions; school publishing programs; interactive media; and merchandise. National Geographic has funded more than 9,000 scientific research, conservation and exploration projects and supports an education program combating geographic illiteracy.

For more information, please call 1-800-NGS LINE (647-5463) or write to the following address:

National Geographic Society
1145 17th Street N.W.
Washington, D.C. 20036-4688 U.S.A.

Visit us online at www.nationalgeographic.com

For information about special discounts for bulk purchases, please contact National Geographic Books Special Sales: ngspecsales@ngs.org

For rights or permissions inquiries, please contact National Geographic Books Subsidiary Rights: ngbookrights@ngs.org

ISBN: 978-1-4262-0545-3
ISBN: 978-1-4262-0751-8 (exhibition edition)

Printed in U.S.A.

10/RRDW-CML/1